The River of Death and Its Branches

Showing How People Perish in it, and How They May be Rescued

by

Martin Wells Knapp

First Fruits Press
Wilmore, Kentucky
c2015

asburyseminary.edu
800.2ASBURY
204 North Lexington Avenue
Wilmore, Kentucky 40390

First Fruits
THE ACADEMIC OPEN PRESS OF ASBURY SEMINARY

First Fruits Press
The Academic Open Press of Asbury Theological Seminary
204 N. Lexington Ave., Wilmore, KY 40390
859-858-2236
first.fruits@asburyseminary.edu
asbury.to/firstfruits

WRECKED OR RESCUED--WHICH?

By MARTIN WELLS KNAPP.

THE RIVER OF DEATH

AND ITS BRANCHES.

SHOWING

HOW PEOPLE PERISH IN IT, AND HOW THEY
MAY BE RESCUED.

BY

MARTIN WELLS KNAPP,

Editor of The Revivalist, and Author of "Christ Crowned Within,'
"Out of Egypt Into Canaan," "Revival Tornadoes,"
"Impressions," "Double Cure," "Lightning
Bolts from Pentecostal Skies,"
Etc., Etc.

M. W. KNAPP,
Publisher of Gospel Literature,
OFFICE OF THE REVIVALIST, CINCINNATI, O.

TABLE OF CONTENTS.

THE RIVER OF DEATH.

CHAPTER I.

GOD'S LAW.

"My little children, these things write I unto you, that ye may not sin."—I. John ii. 1.

"For whosoever shall keep the whole law, and yet stumble in one point, he is become guilty of all."—James ii. 10.

The preceding Chart represents this Law broken, influences leading to breaking it, and the terrible consequences of living in Sin.

Every law which God has made is good, and not one of them can be disobeyed without destroying the soul, injuring God's kingdom, and defying Him; for He has said: *"The soul that sinneth it shall die."*

The Law has been compared to a looking-glass, by gazing into which we may see the kind of persons we really are. If one is a sinner, this glass shows the soul covered with the dirt of sin.

A looking-glass is not made to wash the face; but it does show the dirt. So the Law can save no one, nor make clean, but reveals the uncleanness which Jesus stands ready to wash away.

The River of Death and all its Branches, shown on the Chart, are filthy Streams, flowing through the Malarious Land of Sin, and all who are drifting in them will perish forever unless they come to Jesus and wash and be clean.

We must remember that the love of God is shown just as really in the giving of the Law as in the giving of His Son and of His Spirit.

Sinai is as really divine as Calvary.

The Law forbids Idolatry, because children should love and obey and worship their Heavenly Father above all others.   This is for their good as well as for His glory.

It forbids Profanity, because it is wrong for people to speak disrespectfully of Him who made them.

It forbids Sabbath Breaking, because God loves His children and knows they need a weekly Day of Rest.

It forbids Disobedience to Parents, because Obedience is the corner-stone of lives of usefulness and happiness here and enjoyment hereafter.

It forbids Murder, because God loves people, and would not have them suddenly summoned by each other to meet Death, and if obedient will protect them from every hostile hand until He shall call them home.

It forbids Adultery, because lust is ruinous to both soul and body—to the individual and to society—and He would have His children pure.

It forbids Stealing, because He loves His children and would protect them in the property interests which He intrusts to their care.

It forbids Lying, because it is Satanlike and imperils person and property, both of which are precious in His sight.

It forbids Covetousness, because it is a soul cancer which leads to pride and false ambition, and many other sins which are ruinous to the soul.

In fact, GOD FORBIDS ALL SIN, because it imparts to its possessor the very character of Satan, unfitting for usefulness and enjoyment in this world and in the world to come.

Let us then be thankful to the Heavenly Father, who thus warns us of the Burning Fires of Sin, which will torture all who handle them.

CHAPTER II.

"For the wages of sin is death."—Rom. vi. 23.

This book is a description of the River of Death, its Branches and its dangers, and how to escape them. Study the foregoing picture of it very carefully, as it will be often referred to.

It is located in the Land of Sin, better known by some as the Land of Selfishness and by others as the Land of Unbelief. This Land is infested by ravenous wild beasts and venomous serpents, and abounds with sterile deserts and deadly swamps. Pitfalls and quicksands also are numerous. Its inhabitants were lured into it by Satan, and multitudes have perished and are perishing in spite of the heroic efforts put forth by the King of Heaven and His Son to rescue them. The River of Death, with its Tributaries, flows through this Land, and all its dwellers are borne by it over the Falls of Eternal Despair.

It is an old River, one of the very oldest in all this World. It had its source way back in the Garden of Eden when our first parents fell into its fatal flood and lost their spiritual lives.

It is a deep River, so deep that all who sink in it do so to rise no more, unless rescued by Divine

8

Power. Its banks are so high and steep that no one has ever been able unaided to climb them, and millions of souls have been lost in it.

It is a popular River — not with the King of Heaven nor His Son nor His Spirit nor His people, but with Satan and the multitudes he deceives.

It is a fascinating River, so fascinating that, though its people know their peril and final doom, yet they often resist every appeal and disregard every warning for the momentary pleasure or profit of the ride upon its bosom. They are all the victims of a sort of spiritual insanity, by which the will and affections are deranged and domineer over the reason and the judgment.

It is a swift River. Its current is so strong that no one unaided can resist it, and its waters and banks are infested with poisonous serpents, that sting and hiss and kill.

It finally leaps over the greatest Falls in all the wide World — the Falls of Eternal Despair — and sweeps its victims into the bottomless Ocean of a burning Hell where they are "tormented day and night for ever and ever."

There is no other stream in all the Universe whose currents thus fill the Ocean of Eternal Doom. Hence Satan, himself, takes great delight in it; superintends it from the beginning to the end, and with his imps sets multitudes of baits and snares to induce people to venture upon its treacherous bosom.

It is a deceptive River, and he has a way of making its waters look beautiful and attractive in order to

lure victims to set sail upon them. Satan has a
powder named "Delusion," which makes its travelers
believe they are safe and on their way to Heaven.
He has many agents who administer this powder.

Satan tells people they can have much more enjoyment by being their own pilots and sailing there, than
by getting into the Life Boat, accepting Jesus as their
Pilot, and being landed on the Plains of Regeneration, and carried hence to Holiness Heights and
finally into Heaven to spend a glorious Eternity.

Millions have believed his lies and perished. Many
think they will sail for a "little while only" and then
return; but too late they find the current so swift
they can not resist it, and so sweep over the merciless
Falls, stung by many a scorpion of sin, and shrieking:
"'Too late! Too late! I am lost! I am lost!'"

"To be forewarned is to be forearmed." Hence
God has told us all about this River in His Word ; all
about the heroic expedition of His Son from Glory's
dazzling heights to earth's dark night to rescue
souls from Satan's power, from this River's awful
flood, and the fearful Falls of Eternal Despair, and
the burning lake of Hell beyond.

Would you like to know more about it ? Then
read the following chapters. Before you read promise
me one thing, namely: If you find you have been deceived and are drifting on this fatal Stream, that you
will cry to God for help; break away from the enchanted
spell that Satan may have thrown around you, and leap
into the Life Boat of Salvation which the Saviour
brings to your side. What say you ?

CHAPTER III.

"**Thou shalt have none other gods before me.**"—Ex. xx. 3.

Idolatry is the name of the first Stream that we will notice which feeds the River of Death. Many think that all Idolators are in heathen lands and bow down to gods of wood and stone, but this is a mistake, for ALL ARE IDOLATORS WHO LOVE ANYONE OR ANYTHING MORE THAN THEY LOVE GOD.

The following are some of the Idols which boys and girls frequently worship, and do not seem to realize their sin and danger :

1. The Love of Self. If you love Self more than you love Jesus, then Self has become your Idol. Do you spend more time thinking about Self, admiring Self and looking at Self than you do in prayer? When Self is crossed, do you feel vexed? Does it make you jealous when your brother or sister or playmate receives favors or gifts and you do not? If so, then you are seeking the Kingdom of Self instead of seeking the Kingdom of God, and in the Death Boat of Self-Idolatry you are drifting and sinking towards your doom.

2. Friends. You ought to love your father and

your mother, your brothers and sisters, your friends
and your foes, but if you love anyone more than
you love Jesus, then that one becomes your Idol.
People may become Idolators by allowing infatuation
to lead to marriage with the ungodly.   The object of
your affections thus becomes your Idol, for God forbids such marriages.   See II. Cor. vi. 14 ; also my
book on ''Impressions.''   Do you take greater delight in pleasing your friends than in pleasing God ?
Does it rejoice you more to give to them than to give
to the suffering cause of Jesus ?   If God takes your
loved ones to Himself, do you rebel and feel hard
toward Him for so doing ?   If any of these things are
true, then you have set up an Idol in your heart
where Christ alone should reign.

3. Business.   Many grown people make this an
Idol which they worship.   They give their lives to
their own Business and little or nothing to God's
Business.   They say their Business must be attended
to, and so neglect their souls and the worship of God
who made them, for their Business.   This has proven
one of the most successful Boats on which Satan has
shipped multitudes over the Fatal Falls.   Beware,
children, as you older grow, lest you enter in.   Good
Business is all right, if done rightly and for God ;
but if its claims are pressed before His it is a curse
instead of a blessing.

4. Worldly Pleasure.   God gives all His true
children Pleasures for evermore.   He makes their
peace like a river, and fills them with the fulness of
His joy.   Satan has his sham Pleasures, which amuse

for a little time and then die out and leave a fatal burn. One of the positive proofs that millions are drifting down this awful stream is that they are "lovers of Pleasure more than lovers of God." Do you love your own Pleasure more than you love to please Jesus? Do you play when Duty says study, or help papa or mamma? If so, beware! Many have floated down this Stream so far that they love to visit and go on excursions on the holy Sabbath day instead of worship in the house of God. They love the theater, the dance, worldly songs, the circus, playing cards, and other wicked amusements more than they love communion with God and the company of His people and songs of salvation. They are thoughtless, worldly, gay and giddy, forgetful that they are drifting toward the Falls, and that an awful Eternity is just before them. Like Belshazzar of old, their Pleasure is short and doom certain. Have you not read, in the Bible, how he sailed down this River in the Boat of Worldly Pleasure? How quickly it capsized and drifted over the Falls of Eternal Despair? All who sail in it, unless rescued by Saving Grace, will suffer similar wreckage. Many other gaily painted Boats drift down this black Stream. Some love their Reputation more than God, and care more about what men think of them than what God thinks. All who do so, make that their Idol. Others give greater honor to their own Views than they do to God and His Word. Such worship their own Opinions. In fact, everyone who has not given up all Sin, and yielded to Jesus and been converted, loves someone or something more than God, and hence is drifting down this merciless River. The awful wickedness of this Sin is seen from the following facts:

God has made us, redeemed us, and keeps us every moment, and gives us every blessing which we have. Therefore we should love Him and serve Him above all else.

He has made us for His own glory, and demands that we give Him our first and greatest love. To refuse to do this would be like plucking the sun from the heavens and leaving darkness in its place.

Did you ever think how badly it would make your parents feel if they should discover that you are loving their gifts more than you love them?

What would you think of a kingdom that would drive a kind, good king from the throne and put a wicked person in his place, and obey and worship him? Yet all do this who break the First Commandment and dare to sail down this black River of Idolatry, which bears all upon its bosom into the River of Death and over the Fatal Falls.

If you break this Commandment, and love someone or something more than you love God, you defy His love and authority; you lose His help; you discard His salvation, holiness and heaven, and choose to drift down to Christless, endless, hopeless, awful Night.

If you are in this River will you not just now give up all Sin, submit to Jesus, trust Him to save you, call earnestly to God for help, and thus leap into the

Life Boat? Then Jesus will enter your heart and show you how to so die to every Idol and trust Him that He will cleanse your heart from all Sin and abide in it forever. Are you not ready to say:

" The dearest Idol I have known,
    Whate'er that Idol be,
  Just now I tear it from Thy throne,
    And worship only Thee " ?

CHAPTER IV.

" Thou shalt not make unto thee a graven image, nor the likeness of any form that is in heaven above, or that is in the earth beneath, or that is in the water under the earth: thou shalt not bow down thyself unto them, nor serve them: for I the Lord thy God am a jealous God, visiting the iniquity of the fathers upon the children, upon the third and upon the fourth generation of them that hate me; and shewing mercy unto thousands, of them that love me and keep my commandments."—Ex. xx. 4–6.

The First Commandment forbids all internal or heart Idolatry. The Second, all external Idolatry. One is against treason towards God in the heart, the other against hoisting the traitor's flag and proclaiming it.

God looks upon Idolatry as one of the vilest sins that can be committed against Him.

It is so awful in His sight that He commanded people who were found guilty of it to be stoned to death, and in Rev. xxi. 8 He declares of all Idolaters:

"Their part shall be in the lake that burneth with fire and brimstone; which is the second death."

All are guilty of this wickedness who do the following things:

Who make gods of stone or wood or clay or anything else, and worship them.

Who dedicate temples to other than the true God.

Who build costly churches to feed human pride and ambition, instead of for the glory of God.

Who offer prayers and sacrifices to other than the God of Heaven.

Who worship images of Mary or of the saints.

The following are some of the reasons why all should avoid this crime:

God has expressly forbidden it.

It is a public declaration of the rejection of the true God and the acceptance of sham religion.

It is degrading to all who are guilty of it, as one can not rise higher than the object of his worship.

It confirms its victim in his error. It dethrones the true God from His place of worship in the human soul and puts a base substitute in His stead.

It never satisfies the cravings of an immortal soul.

It brings disappointment and chagrin, displeasure of the true God, exclusion from Heaven, and eternal torment.

This Stream is one of the largest Rivers which sweep into the River of Death. Whole nations are drifting upon its bosom.

The condition of its victims is the more deplorable because by this act of treason against the true God and His Son, Jesus Christ, they shut themselves out

of pardon, help, and Heaven, and throw the doors
of their souls wide open to all the follies and super-
stitions and vices with which Satan delights to deceive
them.

God commands His people to herald and proclaim
to these darkened ones the "glad tidings of great
joy," that they may "turn from these idols to serve
the living and true God, and wait for His Son from
heaven."

Would you not like to be one of the honored number who will go and tell them? If you will fully
yield all to Him, possibly He will call you to this
glorious work, and help you among the heathen
nations to win multitudes to Jesus, and be among the
number of whom He has said:

**"They that be wise shall shine as the brightness
of the firmament; and they that turn many to righteousness as the stars for ever and ever."—Dan. xii. 3.**

People who are converted from Idolatry often
become the very best of Christians.

I have heard of two little boys in China who had
given up all their Idols and were fully following Jesus.
They were bitterly persecuted both by their teacher
and by their playmates, who were heathen. Finally
the teacher commanded these two boys to stand up
before the school, and all the other pupils marched
around the room, and every one of them spit on their
faces. The little heroes did not flinch nor complain,
but broke out in a triumphant song:

" Must Jesus bear the cross alone,
And all the world go free ?
No, there's a cross for everyone,
And there's a cross for me.

" The consecrated cross I 'll bear,
Till death shall set me free,
And then go home my crown to wear,
For there's a crown for me."

Do you believe that you would have been as brave? Surely you may if, like them, your trust is in the living God.

Having read these two chapters, can you look right up into the face of God and say: "Heavenly Father, I have renounced every Idol that was in my heart, and every Idol that was outside of it "?

Woe unto all who are drifting down either of these fearful Streams toward the Falls of Eternal Despair.

Happy are they who through Jesus have been rescued from their waters, and are rejoicing in the consciousness that Jesus saves.

"Little children, keep yourselves from Idols."

CHAPTER V.

"Thou shalt not take the name of the Lord thy God in vain; for the Lord will not hold him guiltless that taketh his name in vain."—Ex. xx. 7.

This is the third great River whose stream swells the increasing flood of the River of Death. Multitudes tumble into it to rise no more forever.

Would you like to hear the story of one of the first persons who perished in its waters? Then turn to Lev. xxiv. 10–16, which is a vivid picture of the fall and death of one who plunged into this awful River. It says:

"And the son of an Israelitish woman, whose father was an Egyptian, went out among the children of Israel: and the son of the Israelitish woman and a man of Israel strove together in the camp; and the son of the Israelitish woman blasphemed the Name, and cursed: and they brought him unto Moses. And his mother's name was Shelomith, the daughter of Dibri, of the tribe of Dan. And they put him in ward, that it might be declared unto them at the mouth of the Lord.

"And the Lord spake unto Moses, saying, Bring forth him that hath cursed without the camp; and let all that heard him lay their hands upon his head, and let all the congregation stone him. And thou shalt speak unto the children of Israel, saying, Whosoever curseth his God shall bear his sin. And he that blasphemeth the name of the Lord, he shall surely be put to death; all the congregation shall certainly stone him: as well the stranger, as the homeborn, when he blasphemeth the name of the Lord, shall be put to death."

God places a special emphasis against the violation of this Commandment, expressly declaring that its violators will NOT BE HELD GUILTLESS. Like the other laws God has made, it is for our good, as well as for His glory.

Human laws provide for the arrest of people for "contempt of court," who speak disrespectfully of their officers. Much more is he guilty who "takes in vain" the name of the King of kings.

Would you not feel justly and righteously indignant if you heard the name of your parents spoken of disparagingly or used in vain? Then how much more should you revere the name and character of Him who has created you, and given His Son to save you from your sins, and from whom you receive every breath you draw and every pleasure which you have.

Oh, the soul-defiling mystery of Sin, that will sink its victim so low that he will be guilty of so vile a deed!

People become guilty of this Sin and exposed to its awful perils in the following ways:

By profane swearing, like the blasphemous words

which frequently flow from the lips of the openly wicked.

By appealing to God insincerely.

By using "by-words" as substitutes for swearing.

By thinking "swear words"; for, "as one thinketh in his heart so is he."

By using God's name in prayer and songs idly.

Have you ever noticed that this Commandment prohibits not only swearing, but "taking His name *in vain*"? So that whosoever takes "His name in vain" in any way breaks this Commandment, and whosoever habitually thus uses it is drifting on this Fatal River's poisonous flood.

Jesus says that for every "idle word" that man shall speak he must give an account at the day of Judgement. If this is true of every idle word, truly it embraces idle words where the name of God Himself has been idly used. Religious blasphemers who thus sin in songs and prayers and conversation, may be even more vile than those whose swearing is more vulgar. Jesus says:

"Again, ye have heard that it was said to them of old time, Thou shalt not forswear thyself, but shalt perform unto the Lord thine oaths: but I say unto you, Swear not at all; neither by the heaven, for it is the throne of God; nor by the earth, for it is the footstool of his feet; nor by Jerusalem, for it is the city of the great King. Neither shalt thou swear by thy head, for thou canst not make one hair white or black. But let your speech be, Yea, yea; Nay, nay: and whatsoever is more than these is of the evil one."—Matt. v. 33-37.

Reader, are you guilty in any of these ways? If so, stop and think. Consider that God hears you, reads you, sees you.

Don't forget that while you may be thoughtless and gay about your work or play, that if unforgiven, every moment you are drifting, drifting, drifting down this awful River; that you have insulted God and broken His law; that you have brought upon your soul the guilt of Sin and the righteous wrath of Him whom you thus have wronged, and that you have invited a fearful penalty which your soul must meet and suffer for ever and ever, unless you repent and leap into the Life Boat of Salvation.

Of all the sins which man commits there is none more aggravating nor less excusable than this.

It is a senseless sin. No possible profit in it in any way.

It is an excuseless sin, as there is no reason why anyone should commit it.

It is a devilish sin, as it shows that its possessor has the very nature of Satan, who hates God and insults Him and breaks His laws.

It is specially aggravating in the sight of God. All sin is loathsome in His sight, but this sin is the only one in the whole catalogue against which He expresses the intensity of His anger by saying:

"The Lord will not hold him guiltless that taketh his name in vain."

May it not be because this sin committed, opens the flood gates of the soul more fully to all other sins ?

If Satan can get you to set sail in the Death Boat of Profanity in this Stream, he will have little trouble in luring you into all the Tributaries of the River of Death.

I wish every reader of these pages would stop here just a moment, and ask God to help see what every person who is guilty of this sin is like.

He is like a criminal, who would break the righteous laws of his country, and then curse the kind rulers who made them.

Like a wicked boy, who would speak disrespectfully of his kind parents who love, clothe and feed him.

Reader, would you like to have me tell you what I seem just now to see ?

I fancy that I see a boy, playing by the side of this awful River.   He goes close to its edge where the bank is very steep, picking Sin's poison flowers which abound on every side.   Suddenly he becomes angry.   For the first time an oath falls from his lips, and he falls headlong into this awful River.   Devils and wicked men welcome him, and in the Death Boat of Profanity he is launched upon the Stream.   At first he shrinks from the awful curses which he hears, but he soon gets used to them, and is as bad as those around him.   False friends applaud him, and, smoking, gambling, and swearing, together they drift rapidly onward toward their doom.   Frequently Christ and His servants approach him with the Life Boat of Salvation, but he says: ''I am having so much fun, I can't give it up,'' and rejects it, and suddenly his boat strikes an unseen rock, goes to the bottom, and his soul, with shrieks of agony, is borne over the Falls of Eternal Despair. Lost! Lost! Lost forever!

Reader, beware of this River!

Christ only can save you. The Life Boat of Salvation waits to rescue your imperiled soul. It will bear you amid songs of victory and everlasting joy to the Land of Life, from which you may pass up to Holiness Heights, and from thence to the Eternal Glory of the Redeemed.

CHAPTER VI.

"Remember the sabbath day, to keep it holy. Six days shalt thou labour, and do all thy work: but the seventh day is a sabbath unto the Lord thy God: in it thou shalt not do any work, thou, nor thy son, nor thy daughter, thy manservant, nor thy maidservant, nor thy cattle, nor thy stranger that is within thy gates: for in six days the Lord made heaven and earth, the sea, and all that in them is, and rested the seventh day: wherefore the Lord blessed the sabbath day, and hallowed it."—Ex. xx. 8–11.

Satan strives to make people think the Sabbath an irksome requirement by which God keeps His people from real enjoyments.

This is one of his blackest lies. Instead of that, God designs it to be a day in which all may rest, and enjoy Christian worship. In communion with Him and with each other they may thus be fitted in mind, soul and body for the work which they must do.

The Sabbath is humanity's great restorer, by which body, mind and spirit rest and are invigorated.

It is a God-given type of the perfect soul rest and heavenly rest which await all who fully follow Christ.

It is a harbor where storm-stranded vessels rest and are repaired.

It is a temple in which our Heavenly Father meets and communes with His children.

It is a celestial observatory from which one views Eternity and its realities.

It is a training school for this world and the next.

It is our "Lord's Day," commemorating His resurrection.

"If thou turn away thy foot from the sabbath, from doing thy pleasure on my holy day; and call the sabbath a delight, and the holy of the Lord honourable; and shalt honour it, not doing thine own ways, nor finding thine own pleasure, nor speaking thine own words: then shalt thou delight thyself in the Lord; and I will make thee to ride upon the high places of the earth; and I will feed thee with the heritage of Jacob thy father: for the mouth of the Lord hath spoken it."—Isa. lviii. 13, 14.

Jesus named some exceptions to the stringent Jewish rule of Sabbath observance. He taught that it is "lawful to do good" upon the Sabbath day, and that works of mercy, like relieving suffering, are lawful and right. He would have us to be neither Sabbathless worldlings seeking our own pleasure, or bigoted Pharisees bound by the mere letter of the law. We must honor the exceptions in favor of "doing good" and "mercy," as well as the law demanding cessation of toil.

Sabbath desecration is an appalling and general

sin.   Multitudes on every side, breaking this law, are drifting down the River of Death "into the eternal fire which is prepared for the devil and his angels" (Matt. xxv. 41).

The following are some of the reasons why every one should faithfully keep the Sabbath day:

Because God commands it, and to break His law is rebellion against His government.

Because we all need the rest which its rightful observance brings.

Because the penalty of breaking it is eternal death.

Because Jesus kept it, and we should be like Him.

Because we need the instruction and communion with God which are received through His worship.

There are many ways in which people break this Commandment, and thus displease God and expose themselves to the certain wreckage which befalls all who persist in sailing upon this great feeder of the River of Death.   They do so:

By doing unnecessary work on the Sabbath.

By making it a day of pleasure and amusement.

By neglecting religious meetings.

By reading secular papers and other irreligious reading.

By Sunday picnics and excursions.

By needless Sunday travel.

By worldly visiting.

By lounging and sleeping.   The night is for sleep, the Sabbath day for rest.

By writing business letters.

By running trains and printing papers.

By doing secular business.

By going to church simply to see or to be seen.

It is impossible for an unholy person to keep the Sabbath holy. Hence, all who persist in remaining unholy break this Commandment and invite its fearful penalty.

He who is guilty of Sabbath-breaking is like:

A man who would rush from the kind shelter of a friendly hospital to perish on the street.

Like a disabled ship which would refuse to remain in the harbor for repairs and so sink in the sea.

Like a man who would steal the seventh dollar from a friend who had given him six.

Like an engineer who would run his train, when the boxes are all on fire, until there is a wreck.

Like a soldier who would disobey the orders of his general.

Like a person who would fondle a viper in his bosom.

Like the first Sabbath-breaker of whom it is written: "The man shall surely be put to death."

Like apostate Israel to whom God said:

"But if ye will not hearken unto me to hallow the sabbath day, . . . then will I kindle a fire in the gates thereof, and it shall devour the palaces of Jerusalem, and it shall not be quenched."—Jer. xvii. 27.

The following are some of the lightning strokes which sooner or later leap upon those who persist in Sabbath-breaking:

Disregard for God's authority, and the penalty thus incurred.

The peril which attends loss of Sabbath worship and instruction.

The formation of evil companionships.

Baleful influence over others.

The reproaches through all Eternity of those thus led astray.

Overtaxed energies, a troubled conscience, an offended God, severe judgements, a Christless death, the loss of the soul, and eternal despair.

The sin and penalty both are more terrible when the transgressor is a professed Christian.

Would you like to know how the Sabbath-breaker formerly was punished? Turn to Numbers xv. 32-36, which tells us:

"And while the children of Israel were in the wilderness, they found a man gathering sticks upon the sabbath day. And they that found him gathering sticks brought him unto Moses and Aaron, and unto all the congregation. And they put him in ward, because it had not been declared what should be done to him. And the Lord said unto Moses, The man shall surely be put to death: all the congregation shall stone him with stones without the camp. And all the congregation brought him without the camp, and stoned him with stones, and he died; as the Lord commanded Moses."

Sabbath-breaker, will you not listen to Him who says: "Him that cometh unto me I will in no wise cast out"? He is able to save, willing to save, promises to save, came to save, is saving millions, and will save you if you will renounce sin, come to Him and trust Him to save you. *Now* is the accepted time. *Now* is the day of salvation. O yield at once.

A young man sick of his wild career had resolved to live a different life, and had turned his steps toward the house of God.

Just as he was about to enter, an old chum saw him, and prevailed upon him to go with him to a Sunday resort.

On the return home he fell from the train, and was crushed and soon died.

While dying he called for the false friend who had turned his steps unto the fatal snare of the Sabbath-breaker, and as his life-blood was oozing away, he fixed his eyes upon him and said:

"That was bad business, Joe, you taking me away from church. When I'm dead, I want you to tell the boys that it was drink and Sabbath-breaking that did it, and while you are telling them *I'll be in hell, and you'll be to blame for it.*"

REMEMBER THE SABBATH DAY.

Rena Ray, in Michigan Christian Advocate.

A young lad, the only child of a widow, came from a home of beauty and wealth in the city to a rural town in which I lived, to spend the summer, that he might roam at pleasure over the green fields and hills, and receive health from the fresh, invigorating air

He was a sprightly, clever boy, and won the heart of everyone that saw him.   He was always in motion, running, hopping, shouting, and singing, and his power of imitation was so rare that he could mimic surprisingly the birds, lambs, calves, and even the clatter of the mill.   Indeed, every sound that he heard was re-echoed by him, and thus he passed the time merrily away.

I was a year older, and of a graver turn than he, but I loved him so well, though, that I would have spent all my time with him if I could.

One Sabbath morning—I shall never forget that morning—I started out alone for church, my mother being ill and my father abroad.   I walked briskly along at first, for the bells were chiming and the organ was pealing out solemnly on the air; but by and by I stopped to listen to the birds that were singing cheerily among the trees.   While I was listening, the cool west wind fanned my cheeks, and I cast my eyes wistfully over the green fields toward the river and the beautiful hills, and although a still, small voice whispered, "Remember the Sabbath day," I yielded to temptation, and went astray.

But I did not go astray alone; no, I met with Ned Darley, the boy from the city, who was on his way to church, and I persuaded him to go with me over the green fields down to the river, to spend the hours of sacred rest in quest of diversion and pleasure.

Ned loved the river, so did I; loved to wander beside it, to skip stones over it, to watch the frogs, to catch the fish, to wade and to swim in it.   But we had not come prepared to fish, and we soon grew tired of skipping stones and watching the frogs, so we went into the water.   At first, we only waded hither and thither, splashing the water gayly about, and singing and shouting in the joy of our hearts.   But by and by, Ned took to diving and swimming and performing little fantastic evolutions.

He moved about with such ease and grace that it seemed as if the water must be his native element; but suddenly he shrieked wildly, put his hand to his head, and sank beneath the wave.   I was wild with terror, and I cried out despairingly.   It was all I could do.   Alas, I could not save him.

Many years have passed by since then, but the boy drowned in the river haunts me like a specter. His cry rings ever in my ear, and I think ever with sorrow that if I had remembered the Sabbath day, poor Ned Darley would be living now, and his mother would not have died broken-hearted.

Oh, friends, when you are tempted to withdraw your foot from the house of worship, and wander off in pursuit of diversion and pleasure, think of my life-long anguish and remorse, and remember the Sabbath day.

CHAPTER VII,

"Honour thy father and thy mother: that thy days may be long upon the land which the Lord thy God giveth thee."—Ex. xx. 12.

"Cursed be he that setteth light by his father or his mother."—Duet. xxvii. 16.

"And he that smiteth his father, or his mother, shall be surely put to death."—Ex. xxi. 15.

"Children, obey your parents in the Lord: for this is right."—Eph. vi. 1.

If you had a map of the Geography of the spiritual world you would find one of the most terrible Streams which flow into the River of Death is named, Disobedience to Parents.

One of the great dangers of this Stream is that so many children fall into it. In fact, it is one of the very first Streams into which children fall, unless they are very carefully trained. If you have parents who have kept you from its fatal flood you ought to shout for joy and run and give them an extra hug and kiss.

Parents are the natural God-appointed protectors, teachers and governors of their own children. How good of God to thus shield and care for you when you are unable to care for yourself. If sin had not entered the world and deranged it, doubtless children would never have felt like breaking this Commandment. God gives the following promises to all who keep it:

Length of life; live "long upon the land." This embraces an inheritance in the "Land of Salvation" and also on earth with those of whom Jesus said:

"Blessed are the meek: for they shall inherit the earth."—Matt. v. 5.

God's favor—"This is well pleasing to God" (Eph. v. 20).

"The consciousness of doing right" (Eph. vi. 1--16).

Prosperity—"That it may be well with thee, and thou mayest live long on the earth" (Eph. vi. 3).

The only exception to Obedience to Parents is where they command to do wrong. In such cases the command of God is plain, and children should follow His instructions, given in Ezekiel xx. 18:

"I said unto their children in the wilderness, Walk ye not in the statutes of your fathers, neither observe their judgements, nor defile yourselves with their idols."

If parents command to steal, or swear, or lie, or cheat, or murder, or to marry unconverted persons, or anything else which God clearly forbids, their authority should be kindly but firmly resisted, even if punishment or martyrdom is the result. If you obey them should they command you to disobey God, then they would be your idols, and you would be guilty of Idolatry.

Upon loyalty to this Commandment rests largely obedience to government and to God.

Faithful children make faithful citizens and faithful Christians.

"Without natural affection" is one of the marks of apostasy from God, while true religion "turns the hearts of fathers to the children, and the hearts of children to their fathers."

To violate this Law is to incur as severe a penalty as of any other of the Commandments.

Children break it and fall into the River in the following ways:

By open disobedience.

By disregarding their parents' wishes.

By treating their counsels lightly.

By being unthankful for their favors.

By being disrespectful and saucy to them.

By calling them "the old folks" or kindred unseemly names.

By jesting about their old-fashioned ways or speeches.

By being ashamed of their company.

By neglecting them when in need.

By living so as to bring a reproach upon them.

By joining in conversation against them.

By refusing to ask forgiveness when they have wronged them.

By giving to others the love and honor and obeui-ence which is due their parents only.

By being discontented with them.

By running away from home.

In these and other ways this Law may be violated and its awful penalty incurred.

Among the results of its violation are the following:

A guilty conscience.

Disrespect for all law and restraint.

Yielding to other sins.

Trouble and disappointment.

An offended God.

Unless rescued by the Life-boat of Salvation, an endless hell.

A disobedient child is like—

A serpent which stings the man who saves it.

A man who turns traitor to the government which protects him.

A lunatic who would burn the house that shelters him.

A man who would sow brambles and look to reap grain.

All who claim the salvation which makes the keeping of this and all the other Commandments a delight shall live long '' upon the land which the Lord thy God giveth '' and shall be like the ''sun when he goeth forth in his might.''

Jesus was subject to His parents when a child, and among His last acts He provided for His aged mother.

Happy are they who follow in His steps.

JOHNNY'S OWN WAY.

Selected.

Johnny wanted very much to "help" his mother bake pies one morning. So she gave him a piece of dough, the cover of a starch box for a pastry board, and a clothes pin for a rolling pin. When he had rolled so hard that his face was very red, he put his little pie on the stove hearth to bake; and then he saw the pretty soft steam puffing out of the kettle. He tried to catch it in his hand, but it flew away. Then he put his finger near the nose of the kettle. His mother saw him and cried:

"Oh, Johnny, take care, or you'll burn your fingers, my dear!"

"Steam can't burn!" cried Johnny. "Only fire burns."

"You must not try it. Believe me, it will burn you. Do stop, Johnny!"

"Oh, dear," cried Johnny, "why can't I have my own way sometimes! I do like my own way! When I am a big man I mean to stand and poke my fingers in the tea-kettle all day, sometimes, and have my own way, and—"

Poor Johnny did not wait to become a big man to do this; a scream of pain told that he had his own way already.

The little white fingers were sadly burned, and for hours Johnny screamed and jumped about sc that his mother could hardly hold him on her lap

"Oh! oh! oh! what shall I do! Oh, dear

mamma, I 'll never have my own way again as long as I live! When I 'm a great man I 'll never put my fingers in a tea-kettle. Oh, dear, dear!"

Take care, little folks, how you take your own way; there are worse foes in the world than Johnny's steam. Your parents are wiser than you, and they love you too well to deny you any harmless pleasure.—

BENNIE.

Domestic Journal.

He was only ten, and small of his age, but he was a hero, and fought his battle and died a victor before his eleventh birthday. Like many other dying mothers, Bennie's had left this message, "Take care of father"; and Bennie had answered, "I will, mother."

And he kept his promise. The gaunt wolf of poverty was always lurking near the threshold of the desolate room which Bennie called "home." But the brave child would not allow him to enter. He could not do much, but he fought him off with all the strength he possessed. He helped a larger boy sell papers whenever he could get away from watching his father; he did errands; he held horses; he sold apples for an old woman who had the corner stand; in fact, he did "what he could," and trusted God for the rest. In winter's cold or summer's heat he was always to be found at night in the vicinity of a saloon which his father visited. Whether it was eight or nine or ten

or eleven o'clock when his father reeled out, the faithful child was always ready to lead him home safely.
His reward was usually curses, sometimes blows; but
Bennie did not murmur; he would keep his promise,
whatever his father chose to do.

When Thomas Dunn, Bennie's father, was sober,
he seemed to care for his little boy—once even going
so far as to put his hand gently upon his head and
say, with a half sob, as if realizing the child's
neglected condition, "Poor boy! poor little Bennie!"
But Thomas Dunn's sober intervals were getting rare.

Bennie, weary and heart-broken, began to fear
that the wolf *must* cross their threshold, for it took
all of his time now to "take care of father." He
was always staggering around somewhere, or stumb-
ling over something; he seemed to need Bennie every
moment. One day, as the two were crossing the
street, the staggering man fell, and Bennie's full
strength was used to pull him to a place of safety.
In another moment Bennie's feet were crushed out of
all shape as two runaway horses drawing a heavy
carriage trampled over him. He was picked up
gently and taken to a hospital, whither his sobered
father followed him.

Terrible days followed—days of physical agony to
Bennie; days of mental torture to his repentant
father. One evening just at dusk Bennie opened his
eyes, in which the light of reason once more shone.
A look of wonder was on his patient face. In the
gloaming he could see the hospital surgeon sitting
beside him. What did it mean?

"Why am I here?" he asked, his voice faint and trembling.

"You were injured, my boy, and we had to perform an operation," answered a gentle voice.

"What was the operation?" his voice trembling with fear.

"Your feet were amputated, my poor child."

"Cut off, sir, do you mean?"

"Yes—cut off."

"Oh, sir, what will become of father? I promised mother I'd take care of him, and—and—"

"Do n't think about that now, Bennie," said the surgeon, his voice shaken with sobs.

"But I *must* think about it, sir; father'll be under the horses' feet, an' mebbe be killed, an' he ain't ready to die. Could n't I have crutches, sir, an' go an' find father?"

Some one whom he had not noticed in the dusk was kneeling at the foot of the bed; the person now crept nearer, and a voice shaken with sobs said, "You do n't need the crutches, Bennie, lad; father's here, and he'll never leave you."

It was even so; over the faithful child's crushed feet the dissipated father had found his way to the *Cross*.

Bennie died that night. His last words, looking up with a smile, were, "Mother! O mother! I kept my promise; *I did take care of father.*"

THANK GOD FOR MOTHER.

Herald and Presbyter.

After one of the hard-fought battles of the war, a Confederate chaplain was called hastily to see a dying soldier. Taking his hand, he said: "Well, my brother, what can I do for you?"

He supposed the young fellow would want to cry to God for help in his extremity; but it was not so.

"Chaplain," said he, "I want you to cut a lock of hair for my mother; and then, chaplain, I want you to kneel down, and return thanks to God for me."

"For what?" asked the chaplain.

"For giving me such a mother. Oh, she is a good mother. Her teachings are my comfort now. And then, chaplain, thank God that by His grace I am a Christian. What would I do now if I were not a Christian? And thank God for giving me dying grace. He has made this hard bed feel 'soft as downy pillows are.' And, O chaplain, thank Him for the promised home in glory—I'll soon be there."

"And so," said the chaplain, "I kneeled by his bed with not a petition to utter, only praises and thanksgiving for a good mother, a Christian hope, dying grace, and an eternal home in glory."

PAID IN HIS OWN COIN.

If children ill-treat their parents they may expect the results to come back upon themselves in similar acts from their own offspring.

A certain son treated his aged and dependent father very unkindly. He would not allow him to have his meals with the family, and compelled him to eat with a wooden spoon.

Seeing his own little boy whittling one day, he asked him what he was making. The innocent though cutting answer was:

"I'm making a spoon for you to eat with when you get old like you make grandpa eat with now."

Surely "with what measure ye mete, it shall be measured unto you."

"I KNOW A THING OR TWO."

Selected.

"My dear boy," said a father to his only son, "you are in bad company. The lads with whom you associate indulge in bad habits. They drink, smoke, swear, and, I am afraid, they gamble. They are not safe company for you. I beg you to quit their society."

"You need not be afraid of me, father," replied the boy, laughingly. "I guess I know a thing or two. I know how far to go and when to stop."

The lad left his father's house, twirling his cane in his fingers and laughing at the "old man's notions."

A few years later, and that lad, grown to manhood, stood at the bar of a court, before a jury which had just brought in a verdict of guilty against him for some crime in which he had been concerned.

Before he was sentenced he addressed the court and said, among other things: "My downward course began in disobedience to my parents. I thought I knew as much as my father, and I spurned his advice; but as soon as I turned my back upon my home, temptations came upon me like a drove of hyenas and hurried me into ruin."

Mark that, boys, you who think you are wise enough to do without father's advice. Do n't disobey your parents, I beg of you, do n't.

CHAPTER VIII.

"Thou shalt do no murder."—Ex. xx. 13.

God loves everyone. He so loves that He has made a Law punishing with eternal death any person that shall kill another.

Is it not terrible that man who was created in the image of God should fall so low and become so cruel and wicked that, worse than a wild beast, he will take the life of another?

The Stream of Murder that flows into the River of Death is red with blood. Satan delights in pushing people into it, and sets many surprises which lead them there.

God forbids all people from sailing on this Stream. He warns them of the awful danger, and if they spurn His warning they do so at the peril of their souls.

People fall into the fatal floods of these deadly waters in the following ways:

By killing their fellow men, by poison, by sword, by bullet, or in other ways.

By doing this deliberately or in a passion of anger.

By taking their own lives,—suicide.

By inducing others to kill.

By exposing others to needless danger, as David did Uriah.

By shortening their own lives through the use of liquor, tobacco, opium and kindred poisonous drugs. By manufacture, sale or license of these.

By knowingly overworking employes.

By taking human life in any of its stages.

By hatred in the heart: ''He that hateth his brother is a murderer.''

Reader, do you realize that, if in your heart you have hatred toward anyone, in God's sight you are just as really a murderer as though you were convicted of the crime and on your way to the scaffold.

By soul-murder, *i. c.*, neglecting to warn the wicked when God commands it.

" **When I say unto the wicked, Thou shalt surely die ; and thou givest him not warning, nor speakest to warn the wicked from his wicked way, to save his life; the same wicked man shall die in his iniquity ; BUT HIS BLOOD WILL I REQUIRE AT THINE HAND.**"-- Ezek. iii. 18.

Thus God teaches that for souls lost whom we might have saved had we obeyed Him we will be guilty of murder.

By secret sins which sap the very source of life.

By dueling and prize fighting.

By wars, contrary to the New Testament.

By becoming slaves of lust.

The murderer is possessed of the very nature of Satan himself, for it is declared he was ''a murderer from the beginning,'' and God says, '' No murderer hath eternal life abiding in him,'' and that murderers, with others who have broken His laws and rejected His Gospel, must "have their part in the lake that burneth with fire and brimstone." He also teaches that murder is a disease of the heart, as well as an act of the life; therefore your heart must be right in order to save from the disease.

Two little boys were once playing. Suddenly one became very angry and kicked his playmate just as hard as he could—so hard that in a little while he died from the effects of the kick, and the little boy became a guilty murderer, to be borne by the swiftly rushing tide on this fatal Stream into the River of Death and over the Falls of Eternal Despair, unless rescued by Jesus.

I once visited a prisoner who was confined awaiting execution. The day of his death was fixed, and in less than three weeks he was to be launched into eternity for murder. Christian friends had labored with him and he professed conversion. I probed him deeply to test the reality of his conversion, and he met every test. In answer to searching questions he said that he was heartily sorry for his sins, had renounced them all in heart, would make wrongs right if possible, accepted Jesus as his Saviour, felt that he deserved punishment, prayed for his enemies, and had confessed Christ before his fellow prisoners.

He was asked: "If the governor would come and offer you a pardon on the condition you would give up your hope in Christ, what would you do?"

With strong emphasis he said: "*I'd stick to my religion.*"

His keeper was moved to tears.

The prisoner united with us in a fervent prayer, and touchingly asked God's blessing upon those who had brought him to the Word of Life. He was executed in a few days.

Thus, now, as in the days of Jesus, many criminals go into the Kingdom before the self-righteous Pharisees, and it is proved that Jesus is able and willing "to save to the uttermost" ALL "that draw near unto God through him, seeing he ever liveth to make intercession for them."

God will help us all to walk in the light of it. While no one who has fallen into this Stream can escape by his own strength or that of any other human being, yet God can rescue as easily as from any other of Sin's awful Rivers. He can save, He has saved, multitudes of murderers, for Jesus says :

"Him that cometh to me I will in no wise cast him out."

CHAPTER IX.

"Thou shalt not commit adultery."—Ex. xx. 14.

Adultery is the name of another of the black Rivers down which Satan is sending multitudes to doom.

He has lured many to launch upon it by keeping from them needed warnings of its danger.

He has also planted many seemingly innocent pleasures close to its side so as to disguise it as much as possible.

God forbids sailing upon its waters. He does this because He knows its fearful perils and because He loves the health and purity of human beings.

His Commandment against Adultery forbids all lust in thought, and word and life.

People break this Law in the following ways:

By living together as if they are married when they are not.

By secret lustful sins.

By marrying divorced persons.

By lustful looks, lustful thoughts, lustful imaginations (Matt. v. 28).

In the above and other ways, many have entered the treacherous **sin-boat** of **Adultery** and been forever **lost.**

The following are some of the places where tickets are purchased for this fatal ride:

The ball room, the theater, the bar room, and the brothel. It is said that nine-tenths of the ruined characters of New York City began their career by dancing. At private dances and the theater evil associations are often formed, and there exposures of the person and lude allusions awaken lustful passions.

Over the paths that approach this River Satan has built many enchanting bowers, and posts the words, ''No harm,'' on every side.

The following are some of the fearful lightnings that leap upon those who break this Law and are borne on to their fearful future:

A troubled conscience.

The wrath of God Almighty.

Remorse and disease.

Disgrace and shame.

Ruined homes.

A Christless death and an eternal hell.

He who commits this sin is:

Like the serpent who stings itself to death.

Like insects which persist in flying into a fire at the expense of their wings and life.

Like a person who is enchanted by the charms of a serpent, only to be crushed in its fatal folds.

Like one who would drink poison, because the liquid in which it is mixed is pleasant to the taste.

Like a person who, to gratify a whim, would burn his own house and that of his neighbor.

Like the man who was doomed to kiss an image
of a beautiful virgin, and as he kissed was thrust
through with many sharp daggers which sprung forth
from it.

As you grow into manhood and womanhood, beware lest you fall into the waters of this River.

CHAPTER X.

"Thou shalt not steal."—Ex. xx. 15.

The name of the eighth River down which Satan is drifting multitudes of young and old into the River of Death is Stealing.

This sin, like the others which have been named, is so awful in God's sight that he declares that those who are guilty of it "destroy themselves" (Prov. xxi. 7); that it brings a curse upon all who commit it (Hosea iv. 2, 3); that it brings the wrath of God upon them (Ezek. xxii. 29–31), and that it excludes from heaven (I. Cor. vi. 10).

Would you like to know how people were treated who stole under the Mosaic law? The following verses explain:

"If a man shall steal an ox, or a sheep, and kill it, or sell it; he shall pay five oxen for an ox, and four sheep for a sheep. If the thief be found breaking in, and be smitten that he die, there shall be no blood-guiltiness for him. If the sun be risen upon him, there shall be bloodguiltiness for him: he should make restitution; if he have nothing, then he shall be sold for his theft. If the theft be found in his hand

alive, **whether it be ox, or ass, or sheep; he shall
pay double."—Ex. xxii. 1-4.**

Stealing, like all other sins. has its root in selfishness. If we love others as we do ourselves we surely
will never steal anything away from them.

Satan is very artful in his efforts to entice people
to the perilous banks of the River of Death.

When you have been tempted to take something
that did not belong to you, like an apple, or a lump of
sugar, have you not heard Satan whisper, "No one
will see you or find it out"? He would have you forget that God sees you all the while, knows everything
you do, and that nothing can be hid from Him.

Then sometimes He tries to make folks believe
that it is not very wrong to steal little things, because
He feels sure if He can get them to steal little things
first it will not be long before they will steal more
largely.

When I was a little boy I read in a paper the following lines :

> "It is a sin to steal a pin,
> But 't is greater to steal a 'tater;
> He who steals a copper
> Is guilty of a whopper."

Now, these lines are as black a lie as Satan ever
told, for the person who really steals a pin is just
as actually a thief as the one who steals a million
dollars.

No matter how little it may be, if you take things
that belong to other people, which you would not

have taken had their eyes been upon you, that is stealing, and we must remember that it is not only stealing, but that God Himself sees it and that it is written down as with ''a pen of iron and the point of a diamond,'' and will sink your soul into the awful River of Death unless it be forgiven.

It is an awful thing for a soul to be drifting in this Stream, and still more awful to be drifting there if it feels it is safe.

Are you willing to look into this matter carefully and prayerfully, as you will wish you had at the Day of Judgement, and see whether or no you are in this River?

There are, no doubt, multitudes of people who are in it who think they are not. Are we among that number? Let us see.

All who are guilty of the following things are drifting in this deadly Stream:

Taking property from others which you would not had they known it.

Cheating in any way, such as giving short weights and measures.

By adulterating goods.

By pretending goods sold are better than they really are.

Many are guilty of this crime, not only in selling goods, but in selling horses, cattle, fruit, etc.

By needlessly taking the time of others. If other people are very busy and you are idle, and compel them to leave their work and let it suffer to visit with you, you are stealing their time. This is robbery as really as breaking into a bank.

All forgery is stealing.

It is stealing to tell lies about a person to hurt his reputation.

To needlessly injure the reputation of another is robbery of the basest sort, for, as the poet says:

> "Who steals my purse steals trash;
> But he who robs me of my good name,
> Takes from me that which not enriches him,
> But leaves me poor indeed."

Writing or telling things that have been written or said by other people and pretending they are original, is stealing. Jeremiah refers to this when he says:

"I am against the prophets, saith the Lord, that steal my words everyone from his neighbour."—Jer. xxiii. 30.

Preachers, editors, and all who thus appropriate the words of others are theives.

Going in debt without the probability of paying is a very mean kind of stealing.

Using money for yourself that others have entrusted to you in business transactions is stealing.

Suppose one of your playmates sells you one dollar's worth of peanuts with the understanding that you would have twenty-five cents of the dollar to pay for selling them and pay him the other seventy-five cents. If you spend any of the seventy-five cents, which belongs to him, for yourself, you are stealing, the same as if you took it from his pocket-book.

The same is true in selling anything else on commission. It is stealing for you to use money which should be returned to the person who entrusted you with the goods.

It is stealing to take time that belongs to another. If you agree for certain wages to work a certain number of hours per day every day, and then begin late or idle away the time, or stop before the hours are gone, you have stolen just so much time from the person who employs you, and are just as really a thief as if you had stolen his money.

Compelling employes to work overtime without extra pay is stealing. Oppressing the hireling in his wages is stealing (Mal. iii. 5).

Refusing to do unto others as you would be done by, is robbing them of their rights.

Using other people's money without their knowledge or consent is stealing.

Cheating employers out of time by tardiness, or short hours, or indolence, is stealing.

Cheating in playing marbles and other games is stealing.

Gambling and church lotteries are stealing.

Deceiving people, and then taking advantage of them to get their property, or injure or ruin them, is stealing.

In all the above and many other ways people steal from their fellow beings.

Now I want to ask one question:

Is it not just as wrong for a child to steal from parents as from brothers and sisters?

You say, certainly it is.

THEN IT MUST BE JUST AS WRONG TO STEAL FROM GOD AS FROM OUR FELLOW MEN, OR EVEN MORE SO; yet, many people who would disdain to steal from others are all the while stealing from God.

All who are guilty of the following things are stealing from God, and in the Death-Boat of Robbery are sweeping down this awful River to certain death. God owns everything. This earth is His and all the fulness of it. The cattle upon a thousand hills. He who claims to hold property in his own right instead of holding it as the steward of God, is a thief.

If you refuse to use the influence which God has given you over those around you, you are robbing God of that influence.

If you break the holy Sabbath day instead of keeping it as He commands, you are robbing God of His time.

Spending money for tobacco or whisky or other harmful things instead of using it as He directs is robbing God.

If you waste the physical strength He has given you in idleness or harmful pleasures or secret vices, you are robbing God of that strength.

To neglect to give as God prospers you for the support of the Gospel is robbing Him.

When His people refused to give their tenth He sent a prophet to them who said they had robbed Him in tithes and offerings, and told them to restore and He would open the windows of heaven and pour them out a blessing that there would not be room to receive it.

If you seek salvation by some other way than by the way of the cross, you are guilty of this sin, for Jesus declares:

"Verily, verily, I say unto you, He that entereth not by the door into the fold of the sheep, but climbeth up some other way, the same is a thief and a robber."—Jno. x. 1.

Whether that other way be by your good works or self-righteousness, or because you say you are not very bad, or because you have been baptized and belong to the church; no matter what it may be, if it is not by Jesus, the Door, He says you are a thief and a robber.

If you refuse to work in God's vineyard, then you rob yourself and God's cause of all the blessed results which would have followed such obedience.

It is an awful thing thus to rob God. Reader, are you guilty? If so, does it awaken you and lead you to cry out to God for help, or has Satan so drugged your soul with the chloroform of indifference that it does not alarm you, or bring grief over such a sin?

Did you ever before realize that, while you are thinking you are being good, really in God's sight you are a thief and a robber, and instead of your being borne heavenward you are being borne down the River of Robbery toward your certain doom.

Yet remember, even such may be forgiven. Though our sins may have surpassed those of the thief upon the cross, the fact that Jesus heard his cry and saved his soul brings hope to us.

This sin is a hot coal that must be laid aside or it will burn the soul forever.

THE EIGHTH COMMANDMENT.

Florence M. Gwinn.

"Oh, mamma, what do you think Miss Douglass is going to talk about at our meeting next Saturday afternoon?" said little Fay Leighton, as she came running into the sitting-room, where Mrs. Leighton was taking a rest after a busy forenoon's work.

"I am sure I can not guess, dearie," answered her mother, as she tenderly brushed the bright golden curls off the little flushed face.

"Why, about 'Thou shalt not steal.' I am very sure we girls would never think of doing such a wicked thing as that," said Fay.

"Miss Douglass is always very careful to choose a subject which will benefit you, and no doubt she has some wise plan in view, my dear. If you like, I will tell you a true story."

"Oh, yes, please do, mamma," begged Fay.

"Well, bring your chair here beside me.

"Many years ago a little girl went with her mother one day to visit a neighbor. The country where Lilly lived, for that was the little girl's name, was very new, and she had no nice toys like you to play with, not even a rag doll, for her mamma was always

too busy to find time to make one. It was impossible
to buy such a thing as a toy at the country store
where her papa did his dealing, even if they had
had the money to spare. Thus you see, dearie, Lilly
had to be contented to play with flowers, mosses, and
the little acorn cups which she found in the woods.
Sometimes she would play for hours in the sand, and
it was great fun to build a mountain, or scoop out
a well, or make a wide desert, or a little crooked fur
row for a brook. There was no end of things she
could do with the sand.

"Well, on this day of which I speak, Mrs. Beach,
at whose house they were visiting, gave Lilly a little
sugar bowl to play with. Lilly thought she had never
seen anything quite so pretty. How she longed to
have it for her very own, and after while the wish to
possess it became so very strong, that Lilly thought
to herself: 'Now if I put this little bowl into my
pocket and take it home with me, Mrs. Beach will
never miss it, and if she does she will think that
it has been mislaid.' But a small, still voice, which
we call conscience, and which is God's voice in
the heart, whispered softly to Lilly: 'If you take the
bowl it will be stealing, and how can you say your
prayers to-night? Then you will not enjoy playing
with it, for it will remind you of your sin.' For
a long time Lilly hesitated, but at last determined
to obey the voice of conscience. She put the bowl
up on the cupboard, and soon after was playing merrily with the baby. Our hearts are always light
when we do what is right. As they were getting

ready to go home, Mrs. Beach, taking the cup in her hand, said: 'You can have this, Lilly.   It belonged to a little set of dishes mother gave me when a child.' You can imagine how thankful Lilly was then that she had not stolen the little bowl.   It was a lesson that she never forgot."

"Did you know that little girl, mamma?" asked Fay.

"Very well, indeed, for it was myself."

"Oh, mamma, I never thought of your name being Lilly," cried Fay.

"And, dearie, there are things we can steal more valuable than gold or silver.   If we wrongfully injure the good name of our playmates, we steal their good character from them.   No doubt Miss Douglass will tell you all about it at your meeting."

CHAPTER XI.

"Thou shalt not bear false witness against thy neighbour."—Ex. xx. 16.

A Lie is any false statement made with a design to deceive.

Lying is one of the most dreadful Streams which feed the River of Death.

The devil himself is the father of Lies, and all Liars have his nature.

God forbids Lying in all its forms, and the Bible declares that it is an abomination to Him ; a hindrance to prayer, and the sin of hypocrites.

Satan would have people think that there are little Lies and big Lies, black Lies and white Lies; but this is untrue. A good man has rightly said that ''a Lie that is half the truth is ever the blackest of Lies.''

One Lie makes a person a Liar until it is forgiven by God, and washed away through the Blood of Jesus.

As God declares that ''all liars have their part in the lake that burneth with fire and brimstone,'' it is of great importance that we all see to it that we are saved from this awful vice.

It is one of the Sin Boats in which Satan is sink-

ing multitudes in the River of Death, and sweeping
them over the Falls of Eternal Despair into the fearful place where Jesus says there is "weeping and
wailing and gnashing of teeth," where "their worm
dieth not, and the fire is not quenched."

God loves the truth and hates shams of every
kind, and all Liars are shams of the worst description.
We must hate Lies like God hates them if we would
be His children.

As it is the business of Satan to deceive people,
young and old, in regard to this and every other sin,
we will need to study the matter very closely in order
to be sure he is not deceiving us.

The following are some of the ways in which
people are guilty of this sin:

By stating things which are untrue in order to
deceive.

By just making believe for the sake of making
money or making sport, or concerning something
wrong.

By making engagements which they know they
can not keep.

By pretending goods are better than they really are.

Lies may be acted as well as spoken, and an acted
Lie is just as wicked in God's sight as one that falls
from the lips.

By pretending to be all right when one knows he
is all wrong.

By being silent. If you hear a Lie told about
someone else and do not deny it you make the Lie
your own.

If you repeat a Lie which another has told, knowing it to be such, you are a Liar as really as the one
who first told it.

By sending word to callers that you are not at
home, when you do not wish to see them.

By professing to be right with God when not keeping His commandments.

**"He that saith, I know him, and keepeth not his
commandments, is a liar, and the truth is not in him."
—I. John ii. 4.**

By professing to have no need of cleansing from
sin, when not cleansed.   See I. John i. 8–10.

By saying we have fellowship with God, and walking in darkness.

**"If we say that we have fellowship with him, and
walk in the darkness, we lie."—I. John i. 6.**

As people may steal from God, so they may Lie to
Him.   Is it less wicked to Lie to Him than to man ?

People Lie to God when they promise they will
serve Him if He will do certain things for them, and
then refuse to do so.

They Lie to God by breaking the promises which
they make when converted, and by breaking the bap-
tismal covenant in- which they promise to "forsake
the vain pomp and glory of this world, and all covetous desires for the same, so they will not follow nor
be led by them."

People who do this and then go to the circus,

the theater, the dance, and such worldly places, are guilty of this sin.

By breaking their church covenant, in which they have promised to be "cheerfully governed" by the rules of the church and to "keep God's commandments."

By breaking the marriage covenant, in which they have promised to love and protect each other "so long as they both shall live."

By breaking death-bed covenants, in which they have promised loved ones they would lead Christian lives and meet them in heaven.

By promising to do some duty and then refusing to do it.

By promising God to give a certain amount for His cause, and then, like Ananias and Sapphira, refusing to do so.

By promising to preach or go as missionary and then neglecting to do so.

These are a few of the ways in which people manifest the devil nature which sin has given them, and Lie to God and man, and thus drift over the Falls of Eternal Despair to spend an eternity with him who is the father of Lies.

God wants to save everyone from all sin and its awful consequences.

The Life Boat is pressing close and hard to all who are in this fatal flood.

Many who once were Liars have been saved from this awful sin and now are full of praise to Him who has redeemed them.

" Wherefore, . . . speak ye truth each one with his neighbour."—Eph. iv. 25.

ACTING A LIE.

Eben E. Rexford, in N. Y. Observer.

Dolly had been told never to meddle with a beautiful vase that stood on a bracket, over the piano. '' It will break very easily," her mother said. Now Dolly has an intense desire to take the vase down and examine it—probably because she has been told not to do so. One day when she was alone she made up her mind to gratify her curiosity. She took the vase down without injuring it, but on trying to put it back the bracket slipped off its nail and the vase fell and broke into a dozen pieces. Dolly was frightened. As she stood there trying to think her way out of the dilemma, her kitten came into the room.

'' I 'll shut Spotty into the room, and mamma 'll think she did it," decided Dolly. ''and Spotty can 't tell. ''

So the kitten was shut up in the parlor, and when Dolly's mother came home she found Spotty there and the vase broken.

'' Do you s'pose Spotty did it ?" asked Dolly.

'' I think she might have done so," answered her mother. '' You do n't know anything about it, do you ? ''

Dolly pretended that she did n't hear the question, and got out of the room as soon as possible. That night she could n't sleep. "You lied," something said to her. "No, I did n't," she said. "I did n't say I did n't break it." "But you might just as well have said so," the voice of conscience told her. "If you did n't tell a lie, you acted one, and that's just as bad as telling one."

Dolly stood it as long as she could. She got up and went to her mother's bed.

"Mamma, I broke the vase," she sobbed out. "I thought if I acted a lie you would n't find out about it, but I can't sleep for thinking that God knows, if you do n't."

We can not deceive Him.

A LIAR'S FATE.

D. T. Taylor.

God is all-mighty. Were He not so He would not be God. It is therefore unwise and unsafe to provoke His wrath. The sinner, the reviler of the Holy Spirit, the blasphemer, do so and sooner or later meet a dreadful fate. God could forget the strongest man into nothingness in a moment. But when He puts forth His terrible power it is as easy for Him to turn a hundred and eighty-five thousand warriors into corpses in a night (Isa. xxxvii. 36), as to strike dead a lying man and woman in an instant (Acts v. 5–10).

The *Boston Journal* says a man was playing at cards with three others at Omaha recently, when a dispute arose about the betting. The man uttered a lie.   Everybody believed him to be lying.   Very loudly he asserted his lie, exclaiming in a bold manner : "I hope Christ will kill me if it isn't so."   His hour had come.   He dealt the cards to the next player. The hand—his last hand.   He passed the cards to the next player.   The player shuffled the cards and asked the man who had referred the matter to his Judge to "cut," but a look in his face disclosed the awful fact that he was dead.   The proof of a living Christ and an avenging Deity was before them.   It is a fearful thing to fall into the hands of a living God. Beware !

CHAPTER XII.

TENTH RIVER—COVETOUSNESS.

"Thou shalt not covet thy neighbour's house, thou shalt not covet thy neighbour's wife, nor his manservant, nor his maidservant, nor his ox, nor his ass, nor any thing that is thy neighbour's."—Ex. xx. 17.

Covetousness is an inordinate desire to possess. Let us imagine that we are talking to a little boy by the name of Willie, and that he tells us what he knows about Covetousness.

"Willie, what do you think it means to Covet?"

"It means to want things that belong to other people which you know you should not have."

"Please illustrate what you mean."

"I will try to do so. For instance: If papa should give me and each of my brothers and sisters an apple, and I should want, not only my apple, but also to take the ones my brothers and sisters have, that would be Coveting. Or, if I became dissatisfied with my father or mother, and would want the father or mother of a playmate, that would be Coveting them."

"Would it not be Coveting if you should wish to dispossess any of your neighbors of their houses or lands, or anything else they have?"

"It certainly would."

"Can you tell me of any instance in the Bible of people that have Coveted?"

"Yes; the story of Achan in Joshua vii. 21. He Coveted the golden wedge and Babylonish garment, and was the cause of Israel's defeat at Ai, and was stoned to death for this sin."

"Can you think of any instance in the New Testament?"

"Certainly; Judas, who betrayed our Saviour for thirty pieces of silver, and Ananias and Sapphira, who Coveted the property which they had promised to God. It seems to me the punishment of these three persons is an awful warning to all who would follow in their footsteps."

"Can you think of anything God has said about it?"

"Yes; in Ecclesiastes v. 10, He says: 'He that loveth silver shall not be satisfied with silver; nor he that loveth abundance with increase.' He says it leads to 'many foolish and hurtful lusts,' which drown men in perdition (I. Tim. vi. 9). It leads to lying (see II. Kings v. 22–25). Prov. i. 18, 19, shows it leads to murder and deception; Josh. vii. 21, to stealing; Prov. xxviii. 22, to poverty; I. Tim. vi. 10, to misery; Psa. x. 3, declares that "the covetous renounceth God"; and Eph. v. 5 and Col. iii. 5, declare that it is idolatry."

"Very well answered, and in view of these answers I trust that you and all who read this book may shun it as you would a rattlesnake."

As we have seen, in God's sight it is just as wicked as any other sin, and more to be feared, as it is more popular and less warned against.

It is one of the most popular Sin-Boats in the mighty Fleet which is fighting King Immanuel and robbing Him of His ·rights and peopling damnation.

It is patronized by the rich and the learned, by lords and kings, as well as by multitudes in humbler walks of life.

One of the greatest perils of its passengers is that they are satisfied with it, and hence disdain the Life-Boat which the King of Heaven sends to their relief.

Like all other sins, it is rooted in selfishness.

It is the worship of self and the creature which is idolatry.

It is a gilded popular sin, little feared and seldom shunned. The peril of its victims is all the greater, because they think themselves secure.

It is a River whose surface sparkles, but which is wide and deep; its currents rapid and murderous. More people are probably borne down its treacherous tides than of any other Stream which flows into the River of Death and over the Falls of Eternal Despair.

It is as natural to the unrenewed heart as breathing, and finds expression in the following ways:

By an intense desire to be rich.

By love of earthly gain.

By slowness to give.

By stinginess and penuriousness.

By unlawful desire for that which belongs to another.

It often leads to Sabbath-breaking.

Also to stealing, murder, cheating, and overreaching in business for purposes of gain.

Saloons and brothels are kept at its command.

To accomplish its selfish ends it defies God and tramples on the rights of man.

It is like the consumption, in that its victims often think they are well when they are upon the very brink of death.

It makes a man like a sponge, always absorbing but never giving, or like a person who is always eating but never satisfied, and who dies in the midst of plenty. I knew a rich man, a church member, who gave but one dollar per year for missions, and feared that he would die in the poor house.

All of its victims belong to the family of Achan, Judas and Ananias, and it loses none of its hideousness when, as in their cases, it is screened by a cloak of profession of piety.

The Holy Spirit convicts of its danger. Jesus provides a way of escape, and God waits to welcome and save from it all who will accept of His great salvation.

It is a heart sin, and nothing but the Blood of Jesus can wash it away. At conversion it is renounced and suppressed, but like a caged tiger will often growl and struggle to escape. When the soul is baptized with the Holy Spirit, and moves up on Holiness Heights (see Chart), then Covetousness by God's power is all removed, and Heaven-born Liberality and Perfect Love reign in its stead.

BEWARE OF COVETOUSNESS.

Selected.

A man once told me how much money he had cleared the year before and how much he was clearing that present year, and it was in advance. Some time afterwards—he had likely forgotten that circumstance—he said to me : "I can not give as much this year to the church as last year." The more he got the less he had for the Lord. The following spring in a bad deal he lost one hundred dollars or more. No one can "rob God in tithes and offerings" and not pay the penalty sooner or later. "Beware of covetousness."

" **They that desire to be rich fall into a temptation and a snare, and many foolish and hurtful lusts, such as drown men in destruction and perdition.**"—I. Tim. vi. 9.

WHAT IT COST.

Biblical Illustrator.

" How much is that estate worth ? " said one friend to another as they passed a beautiful mansion and extensive and highly cultivated grounds. " I do not know how much it is worth," was the reply; " but I know what it cost its owner." " How much ? " " His soul," was the startling reply; and then he proceeded to narrate how exclusively the owner had lived for one object—to build himself a home on earth, utterly careless of the home on high ; and had died impenitent and suddenly."

———

STOLEN TREASURE.

Christian Alliance.

It is said that an eagle in search of prey snatched a lamb from a sacrificial altar. She had scarcely borne it to the nest before it was in flames, and her young were burned to ashes. A coal, unseen, had been taken with the stolen flesh, and God punished the sacrilege with its own fruits. So, many a home, many a business, many a family, has been cursed by God's stolen treasures, and might hear Him saying, if they had ears to hear :

"Ye are cursed with the curse; for ye rob me, even this whole nation. Bring ye the whole tithe into the storehouse, that there may be meat in mine house, and prove me now herewith, saith the Lord of hosts, if I will not open you the windows of heaven, and pour you out a blessing, that there shall not be room enough to receive it."—Mal. iii. 9, 10.

CHAPTER XIII.

THE RIVER'S RAVAGES.

The following are some of the terrible results which all must suffer who persist in sailing upon the River of Death.

1. The Guilt of Sin. God has forbidden Sin, hence the awful guilt which disobedience brings—guilt so heavy that it will sink the soul into the burning Sea of Everlasting Doom ; guilt so deep that no one can fathom it, and so black that no artist can paint it, and yet so deceptive that its victims unawakened by the Spirit's power, often seem unconscious that it is fixed upon them.

2. Separation. Sin not only brings guilt, but it separates from Heaven and God, so that His presence is no more enjoyed, nor a glad and final union with Him in Eternity anticipated, and indifference or hatred and rebellion possess the soul.

3. Bondage. Satan throws a fascinating spell over all who follow his counsels, and sail upon this awful Stream. He imparts a love for sin and for sinful society which binds them with such mighty cords that none but God Himself can break them.

" To whom ye present yourselves as servants unto obedience, his servants ye are whom ye obey ; whether

of sin unto death, or of obedience unto righteousness."
—Rom. vi. 16.

4. Disease. If people had never ventured upon
these Rivers there never would have been an ache,
or pain, or disease on earth ; but worse than any
disease of the body is the dreadful leprosy of the
soul which the fatal atmosphere and waters of these
Rivers give. All who drift thereon not only have
the stubborn soul disease of sin which Paul calls
"the body of this death," "the old man," inherited
from Adam down, but the disease is awfully aggra-
vated by the personal sins of those who suffer from it.
Another name for this disease is Selfishness. It is
seated deeper than the skin, or the blood, or the
nerves, away in the deep soul-center of the spiritual
being, and like the measles and the smallpox, it breaks
out on the outside, in the form of sinful anger, wicked
words, stubborn and haughty expressions and de-
meanor, disobedience to parents and many other
sins, although in some persons the main outward
mark may be one kind of sin, and in others different ;
but any outer mark proves that the disease is in the
soul.

5. Eternal Punishment. Another of the certain
and fearful consequences of yielding to Satan and
sailing on these Rivers is Eternal Punishment, which
God declares all must suffer who persist in this sinful
course. The River of Death, with its mighty resist-
less tides, flows over the Falls of Eternal Despair, and
bears its victims out into the burning Sea of Everlast-

ing Destruction, from the "presence of God," and
the "glory of His power."

The King of Heaven is warning all who are upon
its waters of their fearful danger and of the doom
into which they are rushing.

All along the shore He has Gospel messengers,
shouting, "Turn ye, turn ye, for why will ye die?"
But many are like the young men who drifted down
Niagara's awful current over its Falls. Friends shouted
to them repeatedly, "The rapids are before you!
Turn! turn! the rapids are before you!" but they
laughed and sang, and continued to drift, thinking
they would ply their oars and stop their boat before
it was too late, but passed on from one danger point
to another, until when they would turn it was too
late, they could not, for the current was too strong,
and they were lost.

Others, asleep beside this River, in some of the
fatal Boats of Sin which have been mentioned on
preceding pages, are like the poor Indian. An enemy
saw him sleeping on the bank of Niagara River above
the Falls, cut the rope which tied his canoe to the
shore, and pushed it out into the surging, rushing
tide. The Indian slept on until awakened by the
roar of the cataract, too late to stop the boat or turn his
course, and was swiftly swept over its merciless brink
to certain death. A forceful picture of the fate of all
who do not heed the warning cry which echoes in their
ears, but sweep down the Rivers of Sin into the Lake
of Fire, where they shall be "tormented day and night
for ever and ever."

CHAPTER XIV.

"God so loved the world, that he gave his only begotten Son, that whosoever believeth on him shall not perish, but have eternal life."—John iii. 16.

Is it not strange that men should be so foolish as to listen to Satan, and forsake the delights of the Paradise which God has planned for them, and with one accord rush down to the Land of Sin, and embark upon its fatal Rivers! This seems too absurd to be true; yet, deceived by Satan, and won by his cunning wiles, they have done and are doing it.

When angels did a similar thing it seemed there was no salvation for them ; but they were at once arrested and confined in "everlasting chains in outer darkness, awaiting the judgement of the last day."

But blessed, glorious, unspeakable "tidings of great joy, to us is born a Saviour, who is Christ the Lord!" "Though He was rich, yet for our sakes He became poor," and suffered on the cross of Calvary that we might be rescued from Satan's power, Sin's River and its awful doom.

Yes ; thank God, a rescue expedition has been planned and sent forth from God, the Father, to save a lost world. What has been done ?

The Father so loved the world, that He gave His

only begotten Son to save us. Jesus so loved the world that He freely came, and redeemed us by His own precious blood. The Holy Spirit so loved the world that He comes unitedly with the Father and the Son to press a campaign against sin and Satan's power, and rescue all who will repent.

The following are some of the gifts which God bestows in our behalf :

His Son, who came from heaven, lived, and suffered, and died, and rose again, and now intercedes at the right hand of the Father for us.

The Holy Spirit, who takes the things of God and makes them plain to man.

The Word of God. This Word exposes the awful conspiracy of the devil to wreck people in the Rivers of Sin, and, having put them to sleep upon its fatal floods, to rush them over the Falls of Eternal Despair to the dark dungeons of everlasting doom, where he plans to torment them forever. It tells all about the expedition from Heaven, headed by the Son of God, to defeat the devil and rescue all who will repent.

Conviction. Drugged by the devil and chloroformed by sin, spiritually weak and sick on account of the malaria that arises from the Swamps of Disobedience, the sinner would never awaken to a sense of his danger were it not for conviction, such as only the Holy Spirit can bring. He applies the Word of God, rouses the sinner from his slumber, and makes him feel the pangs of guilt because of the way he is destroying himself and treating God, until he can rest no more.

The Church and ministry. Under the administration of the Holy Spirit Jesus organizes His Church, composed of rescued men and women, who, animated by the spirit of their Saviour, and mighty through His strength, co-operate with Him in the work of rescuing others. It is of them Jesus says : "As thou didst send me into the world, even so send I them into the world."

Repentance. Even after the victims of this River have been awakened, they would not know how to repent nor feel like doing so unless God should give them this gift ; hence He bestows it. It moves them with all their might to turn away from sin with deep and godly sorrow, and cry to Him for help. They begin to hate the currents which are ever sweeping them downward, and moved with fear, they stop their mad career, and escape from the death-trap into which Satan has decoyed them. Genuine repentance embraces restitution, if one has wronged another, to the full extent of his power to make that wrong right. If some one stole your knife, would you believe him really penitent if he refused to restore it, and kept right on stealing ? If people keep on sinning, and refuse to make their wrongs right if in their power to do so, their repentance is a sham, and but sweeps them swifter toward eternal death. Real repentance means to give up not only one sin, but all sin, with no thought of ever going back to it again.

Pardon. To all who truly repent, God offers blood-bought pardon. Jesus paid for it on Calvary, and it is free.

"If we confess our sins, he is faithful and righteous to forgive us our sins, and to cleanse us from all unrighteousness."—I. John i. 9.

Precious promise! Glorious privilege! Wonderful grace which thus forgives! This promise has been the plank over which multitudes have rushed from the Sin-Boats of Damnation to the Life-Boat of Salvation.

"Let the wicked forsake his way, and the unrighteous man his thoughts: and let him return unto the Lord, and he will have mercy upon him; and to our God, for he will abundantly pardon."—Isa. lv. 7.

Confession of sin. If a little boy has wronged you and will not "own up," you know by that he does not really repent of the wrong he has done you. The sinner, sinking in the Death-Boat, must confess his sins to others, wherein he has wronged them, and his sin to God, wherein he has wronged Him; and will do so, if his repentance is sincere.

"He that covereth his transgressions shall not prosper: but whoso confesseth and forsaketh them shall obtain mercy."—Prov. xxviii. 13.

Faith. To all who fully submit to God, repent and confess, God gives the faith to believe His Word, and the promise is the plank which reaches the Life-Boat. Our feet represent our faith, and we must put both of them upon the plank, and thus escape for our lives.

Communion.   Entering the Life-Boat of Salvation
the soul is welcomed by Jesus Himself, and communion is at once established between them, sweet, rich
and blessed.   The bells of the Life-Boat ring jubi-
lantly with the praises of its passengers, and all
Heaven is full of joy that another soul is rescued.

Freedom.   The chains of evil habits which bound
the prisoner to the world, the flesh and the devil
when in the Death-Boat of Sin, are now broken.

Healing.   All sorts of physical diseases were contracted in the Rivers of Sin.   In response to the
prayer of faith, these may be healed, and the body
greatly strengthened through the indwelling of the
Holy Spirit.   A new body, free from all disease
and all infirmity, even like the body of Jesus Himself,
is promised in the future, when "He shall change
these vile bodies, and make them like his own most
glorious body, according to the working whereby he
is able to subdue all things unto himself."

Full Salvation.   The diseases of soul which were
contracted in the River are all checked at once, and
the believer is given a valuable home up on the Plains
of Regeneration, but a complete eradication of sin
from the soul is effected only through the Baptism
with the Holy Spirit, which transfers the soul to
Holiness Heights, where it lives in joyful spiritual
activity, health and plenty, until it passes into
Heaven.   This wonderful change is wrought through
the Blood of Jesus, and fully sanctifies the soul,
healing its every disease, and making it every whit
whole.   Not freeing it from infirmities nor destroying

its freedom, nor exempting from temptation, but eliminating everything which mars its communion with God, utterly destroying the "old man" of carnality, and thrilling with holy zeal and freedom. This complete cure of the soul is received through faith in Jesus, dependence upon the healing Blood, and complete abandonment to His sweet will in everything, no matter how much self or others may be opposed. Without it there will be a tendency on the part of the soul to return to former bondage, and take occasional trips upon the Rivers of Sin. This cure removes that inclination. This experience gives one the right to reside on Holiness Heights, where there is "select company," "celestial music," "grapes of Eschol," "honey out of the rock," "bread without scarceness," and all the fruits of Canaan. The ascent which leads there has several steps. The name of one is Hunger for Holiness; the next, Determination to Have It; the third, Absolute Abandonment to the Will of God; the fourth, Appropriating Faith. The steps are carpeted with texts, among which are the following:

"Even so reckon ye also yourselves to be dead unto sin, but alive unto God in Christ Jesus."—Rom. vi. 11.

"Ye shall be holy; for I am holy."—I. Pet. i. 16.

"For this is the will of God, even your sanctification, that ye abstain from fornication."—I. Thess. iv. 3.

"If we walk in the light, as he is in the light, we have fellowship one with another, and the blood of Jesus his Son cleanseth us from all sin."—I. John i. 7

" Be filled with the Spirit."—Eph. v. 18.

All who have reached the Plains of Regeneration should ascend these steps at once, as their usefulness, safety and enjoyment, as well as the command of their Saviour, require it.

Victory. Another gift which Salvation brings is Victory. What a transformation from Satan's victims to Christ's victors. Yet this, through Him, all may be. For He has purchased for all through His Blood complete victory over every foe ; victory over our sins and sin ; over the world, the flesh, and the devil ; over wicked men and evil spirits ; over the grave, and death and hell. Complete victory ; Blood-bought victory ; Eternal victory. Then which shall we be : Satan's victims, decoyed by his wiles, trapped by his cunning, stupefied by his pleasures, stultified by his spirit, to the grief of saints and the delight of demons, drifting down the River of Death to shame and everlasting contempt ; or trophies of saving grace, rescued through Jesus' Blood, by His almighty power, clad with celestial armor, strengthened with all might by His Spirit in the inner man, and sweeping on from victory to victory forever and forever ?

CHAPTER XV

" So then each of us shall give account of himself to God."—Rom. xiv. 12.

We must remember that the truths of the preceding pages are all to be met at the final Judgement. We are responsible for how we receive them.

Jesus appeals to us now as a Saviour to "rescue the perishing, care for the dying," and "snatch them in pity from sin and the grave," but soon He will appear with "power and great glory" with all the holy angels with Him, and all must appear before His throne for final reward or final punishment.

All who have broken His laws and rejected His salvation must then hear the final awful words, "Depart from me, ye cursed, into the eternal fire which is prepared for the devil and his angels," while those who welcomed Him, received His gifts, and, passing through the Land of Regeneration, ascended Holiness Heights, will receive rewards according to their respective deeds. Did you ever think that the last day of time is just as real as the last day of school or the last day of life? It is already appointed, the day fixed, and the place determined upon. All, whether they will or not, must appear at that time and that place to give an account for the "deeds done in the body."

Have you ever considered that then every wrong word and wrong thought and wrong deed, if unpardoned, will blaze out before an assembled universe in characters of awful vividness and condemnation? And that from the final Judgement there is no escape and no appeal? You should remember you are carrying one of the two books which are then to be opened —one the book of your own memory, which mightily quickened will doubtless then recall everything in the past; the other the book of God's memory, who was present and knew all about you, and can not forget?

Have you carefully weighed the fact that the decision you are now making must then be met, and that then it will be too late to reverse it ; that as the Judgement finds you, so you must spend eternity?

Have you considered that neglect of salvation is simply buying a ticket on the Boats of Sin down the rapid River of Death to the left hand of the Judgement and a hopeless Eternity, while accepting of Jesus, repenting of sin, boarding the Life-Boat of Salvation, is securing one for the right hand of God and an Eternity in Heaven—to the Kingdom prepared for you from the foundation of the world?

" The times of ignorance therefore God overlooked; but now he commandeth men that they should all everywhere repent: inasmuch as he hath appointed a day, in the which he will judge the world in righteousness by the man whom he hath ordained; whereof he hath given assurance unto all men, in that he hath raised him from the dead."—Acts xvii. 30, 31.

" Wherefore also we make it our aim, whether at home or absent, to be well-pleasing unto him. For we must all be made manifest before the judgement-seat of Christ; that each one may receive the things done in the body, according to what he hath done, whether it be good or bad."—II. Cor. v. 9, 10.

" Seeing that these things are thus all to be dissolved, what manner of persons ought ye to be in all holy living and godliness, looking for and earnestly desiring the coming of the day of God, by reason of which the heavens being on fire shall be dissolved, and the elements shall melt with fervent heat? But, according to his promise, we look for new heavens and a new earth, wherein dwelleth righteousness. Wherefore, beloved, seeing that ye look for these things, give diligence that ye may be found in peace, without spot and blameless in his sight."—II. Pet. iii. 11–14.

CHAPTER XVI.

If I could have the thousands of young persons before me whom I expect will read this book, I would like to ask the following questions:

"Do you not believe it is possible for every child to cheerfully and gladly obey their parents?"

You answer, "I am sure it would be."

"Then if that be true of earthly parents, who make mistakes, is it not much more true of a Heavenly Father, who is knowledge, and wisdom, and love?"

You answer to this question, "I am sure it would be the same."

Holiness is the state in which it is not only possible, but pleasing, to do God's will, and to do it in such a way that "seeing ye have put off the old man with his doings, and have put on the new man, which is being renewed unto knowledge after the image of him that created him," you are able to "walk worthily of the Lord unto all pleasing, bearing fruit in every good work, and increasing in the knowledge of God; strengthened with all power, according to the might of his glory, unto all patience and longsuffering with joy."

God commands all to be holy, and declares that without holiness no man can see the Lord. He does not mean by this that it will be impossible for us to sin, or that we will not be tempted any more, for Jesus was tempted; or that we will not grow in grace, for we will grow all the faster when our hearts are cleansed from all sin.

Holiness is heart-loyalty to Jesus, and a holy life is a life overflowing with the loyalty of cheerful obedience.

Satan tries to make people believe they can not be holy in this life, for he knows if they are they will be far less likely to enter the Death-Boats of Sin, in which he hopes to drift them over the Falls of Eternal Despair.

The work of Holiness is begun in the hearts and lives of all who are true children of God, but until the heart is cleansed from pride, envy, unbelief, sinful anger, fear, and all sin, there is something within that is opposed to Holiness.

Jesus came from Heaven, the angels declared, for the express purpose of saving His people from their sins, and that includes the sinful state here named. He suffered outside the gate that He might "sanctify the people" with His blood, and thus purify unto Himself a people from all sin set free.

"Having therefore these promises, beloved, let us cleanse ourselves from all defilement of flesh and spirit, perfecting holiness in the fear of God."—II. Cor. vii. 1.

That this sweet experience in which the will of God is done in our hearts and lives "as it is done in Heaven" is for the young as well as for the old, is as

clear as the sun from Heaven, from the very fact that
Jesus does not forbid them, but that His commands
and promises are to all who need their fulfillment.

God has given us the Holy Bible to teach us how
to be holy; the Holy Saviour, who lived and died and
reigns to make and keep us holy; the Holy Spirit, who
applies the truth to our hearts and, with Jesus, leads
us into this experience.

Jesus commands it when He says:

"Ye therefore shall be perfect, as your heavenly
Father is perfect."—Matt. v. 48.

"Sanctify them in the truth: thy word is truth."—
John xvii. 17.

And when He taught believers to pray:

"Thy kingdom come. Thy will be done, as in heaven,
so on earth."—Matt. vi. 10.

Then is there any reason we should not be fully
saved?

I fancy I hear some one say: "How can I, with
all my weakness, and all my failings, and all my oppo-
sition, which I have to meet? How can I lead a holy
life?"

Dear child, your mistake is in looking at yourself
instead of at Jesus. You can not make yourself holy.
You can not overcome your surroundings and beset-
ments in your own strength, but He who has all power
in Heaven and on earth, and who comes to us for the
express purpose of doing this, is able to accomplish it.

It is His work to make you holy, and then to keep you, and then by and by to present you faultless before His Father's throne. Will you not, can you not, do you not, trust Him just now to do this?

You ask, "What am I to do?"

When you came to Jesus to forgive you, you repented of all your sins and renounced them, confessed them and gave them up. God promised that if you would do this He would forgive you and remember them against you no more forever and applied to your heart the promise:

"Him that cometh to me I will in no wise cast out." **—John vi. 37.**

After those days of guilt, and fear, and burden, and darkness, and almost despair, you believed the promise and proved the truthfulness of the Word: "He that believeth on Him hath eternal life." You confessed Him as your Saviour, and the peace of pardon came into your soul.

In a similar way, you should come to Jesus for Him to fully cleanse your heart, and make and keep you holy.

If you do not deeply feel your need of this, ask Him to send deep conviction for it, and make you so feel that, in view of the fact that your Heavenly Father has promised and commands it, that Jesus has provided it, that His Blood is the purchase price, and that the Holy Spirit is waiting to apply it, you will resolve by God's grace to have it, and will not rest until the prize is yours.

Then, as God shall apply the tests to your soul, proving your earnestness and determination, bid a final farewell to everything, no matter how dear it may be, that would stand between you and His perfect will, and present yourself, with all you have and are and ever hope to be, completely to God, for Him to cleanse and fill with perfect love. Then, when you have the assurance deep down in your soul that you have done this, you are ready to believe and receive, by faith, the promise that if we thus "walk in the light, as he is in the light, we have fellowship one with another, and the blood of Jesus his Son cleanseth us from all sin" (I. John i. 7).

You must now believe this promise and kindred ones, of which the Bible is full, just as you believed the promises for pardon when seeking forgiveness of sins.

If you really do this a perfect peace, and rest, and joy, yea, even Jesus Himself, will come in and abide in your heart, and make it His home, "breaking down every idol, casting out every foe, and washing and keeping you whiter than snow."

Then you must keep all abandoned to Him, and trust and obey Him in everything, and He will keep you fully saved.

Multitudes of the young are enjoying the sweetness, and bliss, and victory of these experiences, and through Jesus' precious Blood are made more than conquerors.

Reader, are you among this number? If not, will you not just now determine by God's grace to be?

May you never rest until you can say and feel:

> " I rise to walk in Heaven's own light;
>   Above the world and sin:
>   With heart made pure and garments white,
>   And Christ enthroned within."

[NOTE.—If you wish more light upon this subject, and will write to " The Revivalist " office and let the editor know, he will send you free a copy of a little book which God has used to make this very plain to many.]

WHITER THAN SNOW.

Abbie C. Morrow, in Bible Morning Glories.

Snow is a symbol of purity. There is nothing so beautiful as the newly fallen snow, when the sun makes it bright like gold dust and diamonds. Yet our hearts and lives are to be more pure and white and beautiful than the clear, spotless snow-fields. A teacher asked, " How can the Lord wash our hearts so that they will be whiter than snow ? " " I know," was the quick answer of a little boy taught of God. " When you look through a microscope at the flakes of snow, there is a dark spot in the centre of each flake. When God washes our hearts He does not leave any dark spots on them."

In a school in North Carolina the children were asked, " What is whiter than snow ? " One said, " Cotton," another, " Chalk," another, " Milk," but one little one said, " A heart that is washed in the blood of the Lamb."

A little five-year-old boy looked up at his mother

one morning and said, "Mamma, ain't I whiter than snow?" The mother did not answer him, and the child's lips quivered and his eyes filled with tears as he cried out, "Why, mamma, didn't I give my heart to Jesus that day in the tent, and now ain't I whiter than snow?" Dear little fellow, of course he was. When we give our hearts to Jesus and ask Him to make us whiter than snow he just loves to do it for us.

An English nobleman, whose wife was dead, had one little daughter whom he loved dearly but did not see often. The child's nurse taught her about Jesus. The father used sometimes to amuse his little girl by riddles, and one time she said to him, "Papa, do you know what is whiter than snow?" He was not a Christian and had never read our text. "No," he said, "I don't." Then the little one said, "A soul washed in the blood of Jesus is whiter than snow." The father asked, "Who told you?" "My nurse," said the child. The father privately requested the nurse not to teach his little girl religion for fear she would be gloomy, and forgot all about it. Some time afterward the Prince of Wales was visiting them and noticed the child. She said to him, "Do you know what is whiter than snow?" He did not, and smiled and said, "No, what is it?" And the little one said, "A soul washed in the blood of Jesus is whiter than snow." The father heard the words from his child's lips the second time, and he kept thinking about them until he became a Christian, and through him thousands of people were saved. Isn't it lovely that a little child's word can bring people to Jesus?

A poor little black girl, with bare head and bare feet came into a large Sunday-school where the children in their cool, white gowns were singing, "Whiter than snow." She sat still, with eyes and mouth wide open, pleased and satisfied. No one took any notice of her, and during the lesson she lay down upon one of the seats and fell fast asleep. At the close, the superintendent, who was a physician, upon going to waken her, found she was ill with a fever. The poor child had suffered for days without any attention, and, attracted by the singing, had crept into the church because she could go no further. She was taken to the hospital and cared for. One of the teachers visited her. She was always pleased when she saw anything white, and in her ravings was always saying "White" and "Snow." One day when the teacher took her some flowers, with her little black hands she picked out a white one and laid away all the rest. At last she became quiet and ceased to rave, and said to the nurse, "Sing, lady." "What shall I sing?" "Whiter than snow." The nurse began singing softly. The little one interrupted her, "Missus, does that mean me?" "Yes, my child." "Me, a nigger?" "Yes, my child." "Den sing it some more." The nurse sang it again, and then told her how Jesus could wash all our sins, and though her skin was black, her soul could be whiter than snow. She was happy and lay still for a long time. She grew weaker, and one day at twilight she whispered, "Once more." "What, my child?" "Sing." And while the nurse sang the only song the child had ever heard, the redeemed spirit of the little black waif who had no home and no mother, went up to live with Jesus and be happy forever, but He had made her "Whiter than snow."

CHAPTER XVII.

ETERNITY.

Did you ever stop to think about Eternity? **How** long is it?

I imagine I hear some one say: "Why, it is so long that if you should begin now and count every drop of water there is in every river, lake, and ocean on this globe, when the last drop is counted it would only be just begun."

I imagine I hear another say, "If you would take every particle of sand and dirt of which this earth is made and count them all, and stop an hundred years between the counting of each particle, then when all were finally counted, Eternity would be just as long as when you first began."

Both of these answers are true. Eternity means never-ending duration.

Time, with its six thousand years that have passed away, is simply a little comma in the infinite volumes of the great Eternity. It is but a small drop in the boundless Ocean of the great Forever.

As sublime as the thought of Eternity is, it becomes all the more majestic when we remember that every soul is to exist through all its ages. "We are, and we can never cease to be."

Where you and I shall spend that Eternity moves all Heaven and stirs all hell.

Satan is determined that we spend it with him, and through demons and wicked men, and our own carnal natures, is doing all that lies in his power to allure us into the fatal Streams of these Rivers and over the Falls of Eternal Despair, into an Eternity of the lost, where we will be hopeless and Christless for ever and ever. There, amid the billows of that burning sea, whose fires emit no light, and whose flames never tire nor cease, there will be Eternal separations from God and all the good. Heaven, with all its infinite and eternal joys, will be lost forever.

There will be no music there; but weeping and wailing and gnashing of teeth.

Those who have been hated and wronged here on earth, doubtless there will wreak their vengeance upon the lost forever.

Wicked men and devils, superintended by Satan himself, doubtless will "torment both day and night, for evermore."

One of the hottest flames which then will torture the despairing soul doubtless will be that this doom was self-chosen. The memory of sins committed, of Christ rejected, of prayers spurned and duties neglected, like a scorpion, doubtless will sting the soul and deepen its agony ages without end.

It is a fearful thing to be lost in outer darkness; lost from God; lost from Heaven; lost from loved ones, who interceded by their prayers and tears to save us; lost in a black burning wilderness, so far from God's Heaven and His millions of shining, shouting worlds that not one ray of their combined light can even pierce the outer darkness; lost amid the howls of demons, the sarcasm and ridicule of fallen spirits, the fightings and anguish of lost men! All this is awful beyond description, but add to this the word *Eternal* and remember that this means FOR EVER AND EVER, and there is no language that can express the awfulness of such a loss.

Oh, Eternity of the lost! May thy infinite horrors and everlasting anguish of despair move every reader to drop the sins that may be bearing him to thy murderous bosom and heed the call of mercy before it is too late.

> "Lo, on a narrow neck of land
> 'Twixt two unbounded seas we stand.
>   Secure! insensible!
> A breath of time; a moment's space,
> Removes us to that heavenly place,
>   Or shuts us up in hell."

Reader, remember that your decision this very hour may determine where you will spend ETERNITY.

"Then shall he say also unto them on the left hand, Depart from me, ye cursed, into the eternal fire which is prepared for the devil and his angels."—Matt. xxv. 41.

"And if any was not found written in the book of life, he was cast into the lake of fire."—Rev. xx. 15.

But, thank God! there is another picture.

When Jesus threw back the curtain that intervenes between this and the unseen world, He showed us a painting, not only of the Eternity just named, but of a glorious Eternity from which sin will have been

banished forever; an Eternity where there is no pain
nor sorrow, nor sickness, nor sighing, nor tears; an
Eternity where Jesus and His angels, and loved ones
who delight to do His will, dwell; an Eternity whose
music will thrill, and whose joys will fill increasing
capacities with inexpressible delights; an Eternity
where we may fly on errands of light and love, for
evermore doing the bidding of Him whom we adore;
an Eternity amid the mansions whose foundations are
sapphire and other priceless jewels; whose gates are
pearls; whose temple is the Lord God Almighty,
and the light of which is Jesus, our Elder Brother;
an Eternity where there is no more curse, and we
need "no light of moon, neither light of sun, for the
Lord God shall give them light, and they shall reign
for ever and ever"; a welcome Eternity; a blessed
Eternity; a victorious Eternity; an Eternity where
usefulness, and honor, and enjoyment, all unite to
bear its people to heights undreamed of here.

How foolish to barter such an Eternity for earth's
honors or pleasures or sins. Is it any wonder that
Jesus represents the rich man who sold his soul for
money as a fool? He sold an Eternity of bliss and
purchased a ticket to an Eternity of woe for a little
property and a few brief hours of sensuous enjoyment.
Let us choose an Eternity where it may be ours to
speed on ministries of love and light from world to
world and universe to universe, magnifying the grace
of God that rescued us from the River of Death, and
thus transforms. Thank God such an Eternity is real
and near, and may be ours,

Reader, may we not meet there? Whatever else we do, may we live every moment ready for the ETERNITY of those who are enrolled above.

"And there shall in no wise enter into it anything unclean, or he that maketh an abomination and a lie: but only they which are written in the Lamb's book of life."—Rev. xxi. 27.

RESCUED FROM THE RIVER.

V. E. M.

When a child I had a dread of three things,— Death, Hell, and the Judgement day of God.

Of these divine truths I often thought, and the questions would arise—how am I going to avoid their terror? Where is a place of refuge? Where can I find a ladder of escape when this world shall be on fire, and the elements melting with fervent heat?

Through the conversation of my elder sisters, I learned one day, that Christ will come in the clouds with power and great glory; but this fact did not in the least allay my fears, but added *terror* to my deep consternation, for something in my heart told me I was not *prepared* to stand before Him.

From the day I heard my sisters say Jesus would come again, I resolved to *do good*, keep God's Commandments, and live in such a righteous way that I would not be afraid to meet Him.

With conscientious earnestness of purpose I set

about watching my words lest I should tell a false-
hood, or in jest take the name of God *in vain;* with
rigorous care I did whatever deed of kindness came
in my way towards others, vainly attempting by *good
works* too btain Salvation, not then knowing "that
by grace we are saved through *faith,* and that not of
ourselves, it is the *gift* of God."

Several years I stumbled on trying to build upon
the sand, until one Sunday in the Sabbath-school I
learned this *truth,* that "Jesus died not for our sins
only, but for the sins of the whole world."

Doubtless I had read that text of Scripture before,
but had not paused to consider *carefully* the wonderful importance of those words, "the *sins* of the *whole
world.*"

Who could accurately compute their number, or
rightly discern their degree of guilt? How I began to
wonder, what ratio my own sins were to the transgressions of the whole world?

After much perplexing thought, I came to see that
my own were but as a drop in the ocean, to the sum
total committed by other souls, and yet so great was
my condemnation, as I drifted down the awful River of
Death, that I felt that the *blood of Jesus* must have
wonderful efficacy to wash away the sins of the world.

For who can reckon up the oaths, curses and blas-
phemies, the lying and evil speaking, the Sabbath
breaking, drunkenness, frauds, injustice, cruel oppres-
sion, and much other wickedness that abound in the
lives of the children of men?

Surely, thought I, although my own heart is *un-*

clean through *sin*, since on "Jesus was laid the
iniquities of *us all*," my own soul is not *too hard* a
subject for the blessed Chrrist to make whole.

Although I at last came to comprehend these *facts*,
my attention at that time in life was so much taken
up by my studies in school and the practice of music
at home, I drifted along, fully intending some day to
seek the Lord.

But how indefinite was that period of time, and
what a risk for my immortal soul to run. What as-
surance could I claim that God would not permit
Death to come and bear me over the Falls of Eternal
Despair towards which I was drifting. For now that
I had been brought to a *knowledge* of His word of
Divine *truth*, I was in peril of Hell and the coming
Judgement, every hour I lived without a saving *faith*
in Christ.

But God was *merciful* unto me, or I could never
have been permitted to write this testimony of Jesus'
saving *power*.

Of late the cares of every-day life had engaged my
attention to that extent I but seldom thought of the
perils which had seemed so very real to me when a
child.

The last time those *haunting* fears had arisen with
all the *power* of their convicting *might* was while
standing beside the casket of one whom God had
called away to Heaven, in the days of her innocent
youth. As I looked for the *last time* on that still, white
face, about which clung such beautiful curls of auburn
hair, I realized, as never before, that the sentence

of *death*, which an offended God had pronounced
upon *all flesh*, would sooner or later be executed; and
so surely as his *Word of truth* held good in regard to
our frail tenements of clay, I felt convinced it would
also *prove* true of our souls having to appear before
Him in the Judgement.

As I took my last farewell of dear Katie, a hope
sprang up in my heart that we should one day meet
again. That comforting thought stayed my tears, for
did not Jesus say, "I am the resurrection and the
life. He that believeth *in me*, though he were *dead*,
yet shall he *live*"?

By a saving faith in Christ Katie now *possessed*
this promised inheritance of *eternal life*. It only re-
mained for me to decide whether I would *accept* of *it*,
and come at last to be with her again.

This I earnestly resolved to do while I turned and
walked away, but imperceptibly to me Satan obtained
the controlling power over my heart, and led me for
a few months to believe I had no need of being in a
hurry about seeking salvation.

Who can rightly estimate the *patient* forbearance
of the Lord? With what longsuffering did He await
my lagging footsteps? Truly His mercy and goodness
were great towards me, else my soul would not have
found Him at all.

Time hastened on until when sixteen years of age,
I attended a Revival meeting in the State of Ohio.
Not with the expectation of benefitting my soul did I go
up unto the sanctuary. I thought more of seeing the
multitude, than I did of God and His way of salvation.

One night, after the benediction had been pronounced, I stood waiting for my friends to get ready
to return home; while standing within a few seats of
the altar, a schoolmate accosted me with, "Come,
Jennie, *join* the church to-night." I emphatically
replied, "No, I am not ready! Some other time I
will, but not *now*." But instead of accepting *no* for a
decided refusal, my friend, who had lately found
Christ, persisted in her determination that I should
set my face *heavenward* at *once*, as though I had no
more time to lose.

Seeing she would not let me go away without heed-
ing her request, with a feeling of desperation I walked
up to the pulpit and gave the minister my hand. Then
and there the Holy Ghost sealed *conviction* on my
heart, and to my soul I heard a voice speaking:
"Jennie, you can not live in the church without being
a Christian, and you can not be a Christian unless you
get your heart *right* with *God*."

As I turned and walked homeward I began to be
persuaded, more than ever, that *Hell* was a place of
writhing *torment*, for I was aware that it had suddenly
opened before my soul.

What difference to me *now*, the fact that I had
been born and reared in a good home, surrounded all
through life with the Christianizing influence which
only a godly mother and kind sisters can give; the
searchlight of the Holy Spirit discovered to me that
unless I found Christ, and made Him forever more my
place of refuge, I would be lost.

For one long, long night and a day I felt the con-

demning wrath of God resting on my heart. Turn
where I would I could not find comfort in anything, I
could think of nothing but how to find *rest* from the
heavy burden of sin that I felt was oppressing my heart.
Alone in my room after much meditation I discovered
that good morals and works of righteousness which I
had tried to do, would not save me from becoming a
companion of the vilest wretch who would ever go to
Hell.   For although there may be degrees of suffering in that place of eternal fire, our Saviour taught
there is but *one* place of punishment to which lost
souls will be banished.

Has He not declared "that the Son of man shall
send forth his angels, and they shall gather *out of his
kingdom* all things that *offend*, and them which *do iniquity*, and shall cast them into a *furnace of fire*"?

For one night and a day, a day that seemed to be
the longest of all my life, I felt the *awful condemnation* of God resting on my heart.   What wonder
our Saviour cried when He came to die with the *guilt*
of the whole *world* resting on Him: "My God! my
God! why hast thou forsaken me."

What agony can surpass the knowledge that your
soul is helpless and alone, *forsaken of God* amid the
avalanche of *sin* that has fallen with sudden *fury* upon
you?

Who could endure the ordeal, only that the Word
of truth bids us, "Arise! call upon thy God, if so be
thy God will *think* upon *thee*, that thou perish not."

I knew there was but one way of obtaining relief,
and that was to "*believe* upon the Lord Jesus Christ"

—but, oh ! who was to teach me *how* to trust Him for the safety of my soul ?

My sorrow of heart was too great for words; I could *not* voice it to others. Prayer was my only solace. But the more I tried to pray, the farther *off* from God I seemed to go. '' Oh ! hath He not loved me,'' I cried. '' Hath He not suffered and died to redeem such a lost rebel as I ? '' But true as this fact was, I could not *by faith* step out on the *promises of God*—they were so very broad and high my soul staggered at them.

As the weary day wore away and the lengthening shadow's of evening came on, how I longed to hear the sound of the church bell.

At last its tones pealed out in sweetest *music* to my ear, it seemed to call to me of

> '' Peace, sweet peace, that passeth understanding,
> Peace, sweet peace, that has *no ending*,''

until my heart took courage to believe I would *find Jesus* by going up again to the house of God.

That never-to-be-forgotten night the minister preached from the text—'' Yet a little sleep, a little slumber, a little folding of the hands to sleep.''

Never did words of Divine truth so accurately portray the condition of a lost soul as those did my own, for had I not for years been *slumbering* on, intending at some future day to *arise* and seek Jesus, but had still delayed, until aroused by my friend *insisting* that I had *need* to turn to God just *now ?*

What gratitude at this distant day wells up in my

heart to Jesus that he did not *allow* my heart to resist
the *call* of the Holy Spirit, for had I refused to *hearken*
then, I might have died *unsaved*, for—

> " There is *a time* we know not when, a point we know not where,
>   That makes the destiny of man to glory or despair;
> There is a line by us *unseen*, that crosses ev'ry path,
>   The hidden boundary between God's *patience* and His wrath.

> " How *far* may we go on in sin, how long will God forbear ?
>   Where does hope *end*, and where begins the confines of despair ?
> An answer from the skies is sent, Ye that from God depart,
>   While it is called " to-day " *repent*, and harden not your heart."

"A little more sleep," how like dagger strokes
did every word drop on my quivering heart as that
man of God went on to speak truths analogous to
this:

In a comparative sense there are but *few*, who come
to a knowledge of the gospel that *intend* to be lost.

At some future time they purpose to lay hold *by*
faith upon Christ, but not just *now;* not until I see
that *necessity* compels me to make a leap for *eternal*
life, then I hope to make sure of a foothold on the
Rock of Ages.

But know ye not, oh! *slumbering* soul, your days
on earth may be numbered, and the phantom of *death*
may even now attend your footsteps ? Why sleep on,
only to find a rude awakening when your immortal
spirit is sinking down, down, over the Falls of Eternal
Despair and outer darkness ?

Awake! Leap for your life! Stay not to look
around you! Do not, as you value your soul, listen
to the voice of Satan bidding you to longer *delay*.

Just then, above the noise of the rising congregation, I heard the words in melodious song of—

> "Come, ye sinners, poor and needy,
>   Weak and wounded, sick and sore;
>   Jesus ready stands to save you,
>   Full of *pity*, love and *power*."

As the first verse of this beautiful invitation hymn
rolled away, I became conscious of the fact that much
as I knew I needed Christ, there was another force
which held me for a time spellbound where I stood.

Presently I heard deep down in my soul: "Time
enough, no need to be in a rush about starting for
Heaven; wait until another meeting comes round."

But over and above all this at length spoke the
blessed Master: "Come unto me all ye that labour
and are heavy laden, and I will give you rest." *Rest*,
oh! how had I earnestly sought it, and found it not.
All that long, long weary day my heart still cried out
for that *peace* which Christ alone could give.

To halt between "two opinions" *now*, was to be
lost forever. Realizing this I began to think I would
give a great deal to be kneeling at the altar just at
that moment, calling to God to have mercy upon me.
But, oh! what a distance I would have to walk up the
aisle before all that crowd of friends. Was there no
other way I could find Jesus?

Just then the third verse of the hymn rang out in
painful distinctness:

> "Let not *Satan* make you linger;
>   Nor of fitness fondly dream:
>   All the fitness Christ requireth
>   Is to feel your need of Him."

As these melting words fell upon my burdened heart, I felt the Holy Spirit striving again in mighty power with my soul, but just as I was on the point of yielding, Satan—seeing his grasp on me was broken—suggested, "Do not kneel at that altar, but go to the front bench."

This quite decided me, and I started up the aisle feeling I would sink down at every step; but when I drew near the front bench, I found Satan had prevailed upon other souls also to go a little ways toward God, and what was my dismay to find all the places occupied.

But the devil found he had overshot his mark, for the Lord *prevailed*, and I never stopped going until I fell down at His feet, kneeling inside the altar with my face toward the audience.

While I tried to lift my heart to God in prayer, I realized that I was indeed

> "Weary, heavy-laden,
>   Bruised and mangled by the fall;
>   Had I tarried until *better*,
>   I would not have come at all."

What darkness settled down like a thick cloud upon my soul. Not a ray of light could I see. Out of the surrounding gloom to my heart there was a voice speaking: "Look unto *me*, and be ye *saved*."

But just how to take hold upon Jesus and appropriate to my soul, *by faith*, the sacrifice He offered on Calvary's cross, I knew not, and the more I struggled to find Him, the deeper I plunged into despair.

Ere long the devil threw his power over me until
my *sins* arose like a towering mountain above my
head, and I was tempted to believe there was no
mercy for me.

At this, my courage gave way. Helpless, I quailed
before Satan's overwhelming charge; but while he was
following up the great advantage he had gained
over my drooping heart, my dear Sabbath-school
teacher came to my relief. Her tidings of comfort
were:

"Jennie, so long as Satan can keep your mind
fastened upon your sins, you can not think of *Jesus*.
If you are willing to give up *sin*, you have nothing
more to do with it—God will see to that—but go to
believing upon the Lord Jesus Christ as a *personal
Saviour*, and He will set you free."

Finding at length my sorrow too great for words
she went on:

"As you *by faith* look to the cross, *believe* those
dear hands were nailed there for you; *believe* those
feet were spiked down to save your own from slipping
into Hell; *believe the blood* flowed from that wounded
side to *wash your sins* away."

While my teacher thus encouraged me to take
hold *by faith* upon Jesus, the light *of God* began to
break upon my benighted soul, the power of Satan
was broken, and for a few moments

> "I saw One hanging on a tree,
>   In agonies and blood;
> Who fixed His languid eyes on me,
>   As near His cross I stood.

" Sure, never till my latest breath,
  Can I forget that look;
It seemed to charge me with His death,
  Though not a word He spoke.

" My *conscience felt* and owned the guilt,
  And plunged me in despair;
I saw my sins His blood had spilt,
  And helped to *nail* him there.

" A second look He gave which said,
  I freely all forgive;
This *blood* is for thy ransom paid,
  I die, that you may live."

When at last I reached the point that I could, and
did, that moment *trust* in the *blood of Christ*, in-
stantly I felt the crushing burden lifted, and I knew
my heart had been "washed" and made "whiter
than the snow."

As the *saving power* of the Holy Spirit fell upon
me, I arose to my feet rejoicing in Jesus' forgiving
love.

What a transformation had been wrought. My
friends never looked *so beautiful*, and a new light—
the light of Heaven—appeared to *glow* upon the
walls of the church and everything around me.

How much I loved everybody, and Jesus *most of
all*. Oh! that I could bring every sinner in all the
wide world to seek Him for his own.

Now all fear of Death, Hell, and the Judgement
day of God vanished away. Jesus had come into my
heart and taken away all dread of the law.

How I rejoiced that I had been led of the Spirit to
humble my pride and kneel at that altar; now it had

become the most sacred spot on earth to me, for there
I *found* my Saviour. Right joyfully did I join in
singing:

> "O happy day that fixed my choice
>   On Thee, my Saviour and my God;
> Well may this glowing heart rejoice,
>   And tell its raptures all abroad.

> "'T is done, the great transaction's done,
>   I am my Lord's, and He is mine;
> He drew me and I followed on,
>   Charmed to confess the voice Divine.

> "High Heaven that heard the *solemn vow*,
>   That vow renewed shall *daily hear:*
> Till in life's latest hour I bow,
>   And bless in death a bond so dear.

CARRIED OVER THE FALLS.

[We copy the following warning incidents from many similar cases
given in *"Revival Kindlings"* of many persons who have neglected
salvation, and been swept over the Falls of Eternal Despair.]

"TELL THEM MY SOUL IS IN HELL."
Selected.

A merchant once went to the Eastham camp-meeting with his pious wife, who was very anxious for his
conversion. The spirit of the meeting troubled him,
and, after one day, he resolved to leave his wife on
the ground and return home.

"Do stay, my dear husband," entreated his wife;
"you will be better pleased to-day, maybe, than you
were yesterday."

"No, my partner may need me in his business.   I
shall go," he replied.

"But you made arrangements to be away a week;
do stay, husband, and maybe you will find salvation,"
rejoined his wife.

"No, I must go.   I will go.   Indeed, I hate the
place so much that if my soul would be eternally
damned for going home I would n't stay here," was
his awful answer.

His horror-struck wife stood silent.   Then turning
on his heel, he hurried to the shore and sailed away
from the camp-ground.

On his arrival home he entered his store tired and
hungry.   Seeing a piece of bread and butter on the
counter, he ate it.   Fifteen minutes later his partner
came in, and, after the usual salutation, looked round
and with a perturbed manner asked,—

"What has become of the piece of bread and
butter I left here?"

"I ate it," replied the merchant.

"Ate it!   Dear me!   It was poisoned for the rats.
You are a dead man.   Hurry home in yonder hack,
while I go for the doctor."

The alarmed merchant was borne to his home.
The doctor was soon with him.   Antidotes were ad-
ministered, but they were powerless to save.   The
poison was fiercely assailing the seat of life.   The
pains of death soon got hold upon him.   He was in
agony both of mind and body.

"Have you any message for your wife?" inquired
his distressed partner.

This question recalled the camp-ground and the awful words he had spoken when leaving his wife. Gathering his remaining strength as for a last effort, he fixed his glaring eyes upon his friend and said, in piercing tones:

"Carry my body to the camp-ground, and tell them my soul is in hell!"

He sank back exhausted. The struggle was over. His life in the body had ended. His life in hell had begun!

Reader, are you in the habit of trifling with eternal things? If so, let the horrible end of this merchant teach you that it is a "fearful thing to fall into the hands of the living God." Remember "God is a consuming fire." It is not safe to mock at Him, or at His truth. Beware!

MISSED IT AT LAST.

Selected.

Some time ago, a physician called upon a young man who was ill. He sat for a little by the bedside, examining his patient, and then he honestly told him the sad intelligence that he had but a very short time to live. The young man was astonished; he did not expect it would come to that so soon. He forgot that death comes "in such hour as ye think not." At length he looked up into the face of the doctor, and with a most despairing countenance, repeated the expression: "I have missed it—at last."

"What have you missed?" inquired the tender-hearted, sympathizing physician.

"I have missed it—at last," again he repeated.

"Missed what?"

"Doctor, I have missed the salvation of my soul."

"Oh, say not so;—it is not so. Do you remember the thief on the cross?"

"Yes, I remember the thief on the cross. And I remember that he never said to the Holy Ghost—Go thy way. But *I did*. And now He is saying to me—Go *your way*." He lay gasping a while, and looking up with a vacant, staring eye, he said: "I was awakened and was anxious about my soul, a little time ago. But I did not want to be saved *then*. Something seemed to say to me, 'Don't put it off, make sure of salvation.' I said to myself, 'I will postpone it.' I knew I ought not to do it. I knew I was a great sinner and needed a Saviour. I resolved, however, to dismiss the subject for the present. Yet I could not get my own consent to do it until I had promised to take it up again, at a time not remote and more favorable. I bargained away, resisted and insulted the Holy Spirit. I never thought of coming to this. I meant to have made my salvation sure, and now I have missed it—at last."

"You remember," said the doctor, "that there were some who came at the eleventh hour."

"My eleventh hour," he rejoined, "was when I had that call of the Spirit. I have had none since—shall not have. I am given over to be lost. Oh! I have missed it! I have sold my soul for nothing—a feather—a straw—undone forever!" This was said with such indescribable despondency that nothing was said in reply. After laying a few moments, he raised his head, and looking all around the room as if for some desired object, buried his face in the pillow, and again exclaimed in agony and horror, "Oh! I have missed it at last," and died.

Reader, you need not miss your salvation, for you may have it now. What you have read is a true story. How earnestly it says to you, "Now is the accepted time!"

"To-day, if ye will hear his voice, harden not your hearts."

AN AWFUL JUDGEMENT.

The following incident from the pen of Sister M. A. Sparling, Claremont, N. H., is an illustration of the words of Holy Writ, that "the wicked is snared in the work of his own hands." She writes: "While reading 'Echo from the Border Land' something said, You have an echo from the 'lower region.' If it were father's will I'd love to stand up in your congregation and deliver the message; I can only write. A few years ago I was at a camp-meeting in Rockingham, Vt., and a gang of rowdies got together to set a time to break up the whole meeting. They lived eight miles away. So on Thursday evening they came on the ground to accomplish their fiendish work, and have their 'fun,' as they told some of their friends. Their plan was to lay trains of powder into every tent, under the beds, and when the town clock struck twelve, all were to touch fire to the powder and run to a distance, and see the frightened women and children run and scream. At ten, a distant thunder was heard, and while they were waiting for the hour to set fire, God sent one of the most terrific thunder and hail storms I ever witnessed. It had been a hot day and these young men had no overcoats to put on; and as their last resort, after seeing their powder all wet and their plans all defeated, they were compelled to ride back to their homes, eight miles, all drenched with rain and chilled through. The ringleader had to be carried into the house benumbed. His mother tried for hours to get him warm. Then came a burning fever, and then he called his dear mother and told her what he had done, saying: 'Mother, I've got to die! Do pray! Do pray! What shall I do? Oh, how can I die?' She said: 'I never prayed.' 'Then call father,' cried the dying man. He could not pray. Then he cried: 'What shall I do? Oh, how can I die!' Then he would clutch his hands and wring them in agony, crying, 'I can't die so! I can't die so! Mother, mother, do pray! do pray!'

"The father went for a Baptist minister, but before he arrived the boy was insane; and with distorted eyes, hands uplifted over his head, and writhing in agony, he died raving, and among his last words were: 'I'm going to hell; I'm lost! Lost! Lost! I can't die so! I can't! I can't! Mother, 't is awful to go to hell this way.'"

This seems a fulfillment of the Word which declares of the wicked that "distress and anguish make him afraid; they prevail against him, as a king ready to the battle" (Job xv. 24).

"I AM NOT PENITENT."

The following scene is described by Evangelist Caughey:

Upon the bed of his last sickness lay a dying infidel. He was asked a question, to which his countenance replied, before he had uttered a word: "Are your principles sufficient to sustain you in this trying hour?" He answered sternly, "No;" and after a pause, unable to restrain his feeling, he exclaimed, "Surely, I am the greatest fool in the world to have become the dupe of wicked and designing men; I am justly consigned to that hell, the idea of which I once laughed at." Offers of pardon through the Blood of the Lamb were freely presented and sadly and sullenly put away. He heard the exhortation with patience, till "penitent sinner" was mentioned; when he cried, "Penitent sinner! I am not penitent. It is the fear of eternal damnation that is at work upon my guilty soul; this is nothing else but a pledge and foretaste of the misery of the damned. Eternal fire! eternal fire! who can dwell with everlasting burnings? My body can not live and my soul dare not die. Oh, that I had another day! but this would be of no use; I must perish, and reconcile myself to my lot; I am dying! I am dying!" A second attempt was made to turn his despairing conscience to the cross, which he heard with more than usual patience. When the individual ceased, he became very restless, and at last shrieked fearfully, crying, "See! see! do you not see them? They are come for me, I must go to my place." The horror on his countenance was infernal. His last words were, ''Damned, damned, forever damned!''

HOW A YOUNG LADY GAINED A DRESS BUT LOST HER SOUL.

Mary Wheaton.

The following incident was told me by a friend who was acquainted with the circumstances:

A young lady who used to sing in operas and fashionable concerts, was walking along the streets with a young gentleman one afternoon, and they came to a church in which revival meetings were being held. They were not in the habit of attending such meetings, but the singing so attracted the lady's attention, that she spoke to the gentleman about it and said: ''Let us go inside and listen.'' ''You do n't want to go in there,'' said he, ''they are having revival meetings.'' But the longer she listened to the music the more she was impressed with the thought of going where she could hear better, and at last said, ''I am going in the church.'' So they both went in and took seats. The minister soon arose, and after reading his text, preached to the unconverted. It seemed to the young lady that every word he said was intended for her. She was convicted, and left the church with the intention of living a different life. On reaching home, where her unconverted mother was, the daughter said, ''Mother, I am going to be a better girl.''

''What do you mean?'' asked the parent.

''I mean, I am going to be a Christian.''

''Daughter, you do n't know what you are talking

about. You are too young to be a Christian. Religion is all right for old people, but you are just the age to enjoy yourself, and do n't want to think of such things."

The words of the mother did not change the good resolutions of the daughter. She still said: "I am going to live for God." A few days after this, she was called on to sing in a worldly entertainment, and refused because she had made up her mind to sing for God. As soon as her mother heard what she had done, she was angry, and reproved her very severely. Seeing this did not accomplish her aim, she scoffed at her. Then she tried coaxing, and at last promised her a new silk dress if she would do the required singing.

This was a great temptation to the young lady, for she had been very fashionable and liked to dress so. After studying over the matter for a while, she said: "I will sing just once more to get the dress, but it will be the last time." She at once commenced preparation for the singing. As soon as she began to associate with her old friends the desire for religion left her, and she said to herself: "I believe mother is right; I guess I am too young to be a Christian. I will enjoy myself for a while yet, and when I get older I will seek God." How long did she enjoy herself? A week after this she is taken very ill. Then she wanted Christ. The minister she heard preach a short time ago was sent for. He and a few Christian friends came and prayed for her. She, too, plead for salvation, but finally said: "It is no use, I have put off serving God too long—I can see the very gates of hell open to receive me." She then spoke to her mother and said: "Get me my new silk dress." After hesitating a few minutes the mother did so, and as she brought it near, the daughter said: "Hang it up there," pointing to a hook near the bed. After the dress was hung on the hook, she pointed to it and said: "Mother, that is the price of my soul," and passed into an endless eternity.

"What doth it profit a man, to gain the whole world, and forfeit his life?" (Mark viii. 36.)

WHY WILL YE DIE?

W. H. S.; Arranged.

When the cold, clammy hand of your enemy Death,
Has silenced your heart and suspended your breath,
When friends, bowed in grief, your dead body surround,
O where, careless one, will your poor soul be found?

Deep down in the HELL where all Christless ones go,
Immersed in DESPAIR and surrounded with woe,
Your soul will be wailing, and joining its cry
With the groans of the lost as they bitterly sigh.

In HELL, where the flames will FOREVER be fierce;
In HELL, where the fangs of the worm EVER pierce;
In HELL, where the torments have NEVER an end;
In HELL, where the wicked in anguish descend.

Then hurried along on the fiery wave,
No eye to take pity, and NO ONE TO SAVE;
Fierce fiends will attend as you go wailing by,
And laugh at your anguish, and mock your sad cry.

FOR EVER AND EVER deep down in the fire,
Your woes will increase, and your moans will rise
      higher,
The smoke of your torment will mount like a cloud,
And will wrap you around in its terrible shroud.

Then thinking of folly that merits your doom,
Of Christ who once knocked, but was given NO ROOM,
You'll PRAY, in despair by agony driven,
But prayer said in Hell, can never reach Heaven.

The flames WILL NOT SLACK, growing hotter and fierce,
And the tooth of the worm still DEEPER will pierce;
Your cry WILL NOT RISE from the caverns of Hell,
But echo around where the dark demons dwell.

Salvation was FREE, but you clung to your sin;
And God WOULD HAVE SAVED, had you yielded to Him.
His Spirit oft strove, but you said to Him, "Go,"
And now you're in Hell, 'mid its anguish and woe.

But WHY should you perish, SINCE JESUS HAS DIED—
Since life has flowed out from His spear-pierced side,
Your vast load of guilt was all LAID UPON HIM.
Who finished the work and atoned for your sin?

There's naught can avail, that you ever can do,
But repent and believe in His promise so true,
Oh, COME AS A SINNER, deserving of Hell,
Trust Christ as YOUR Saviour, and all will be well.

Yes, still there is MERCY, and wide stands the gate,
While Jesus implores, and continues to wait:
"O come UNTO ME; quickly come and be blest;
In ME there is safety, in ME there is rest."

Refuse not this message; 't is sent you from Heaven,
It MAY BE THE LAST that to you will be given!
O LOOK to the Saviour; yes, look to Him now;
Accept Him at once, and in penitence bow.

THE END.

"WRECKED or RESCUED?"

A Striking⸺

Salvation Wall Chart.

By the Editor of The Revivalist.

22x28—Tinned For Hanging,

LITHOGRAPHED IN SEVEN COLORS.

It forcefully pictures the River of Death sweeping its multitudes in the "Death Boats of Sin" past the "Lighthouses of Salvation" over the frightful "Falls of Eternal Despair." Also, tributary streams which feed the "River of Death;" "Plains of Regeneration," "Holiness Heights" and "Heaven." It is

A Mighty Silent Preacher.

It warns of sin and convicts for Full Salvation.

Its silent arguments are unanswerable.

It will enable you to preach to your family and visitors in a way that you can not afford to miss.

At a large expense it has been prepared by an expert artist and skillful lithographers, and will be an edifying ornament, framed, or as a wall chart, in any home.

Price, postpaid, 60 cents.

TO REVIVALIST SUBSCRIBERS:

Subscribers for the Weekly Revivalist can have this Chart postpaid by adding only 25 cents.

TOTAL, $1.25.

A Gold Mine for Agents
and Book Evangelists.

Will Sell at Sight.
Write for terms.

M. W. KNAPP,

REVIVALIST OFFICE,   CINCINNATI, O.

THE REVIVALIST.

A FULL SALVATION JOURNAL,

Published WEEKLY in the interest of

THE KINGDOM OF HEAVEN.

FREE FROM QUESTIONABLE ADVERTISEMENTS.

Pentecostal.　　　　Missionary.

Loyal.　　　　　　Evangelical.

"In essentials, unity; in non-essentials, liberty; in all
things, charity."

GOD, WHOM WE SERVE,　　-　　　　　Proprietor.

M. W. KNAPP, -　　-　　-　　-　　　　Editor.

SETH C. REES,　　-　　-　　　-　　-　Associate.

W. N. HIRST,　-　　-　　-　　Book Department.

BYRON J. REES,　-　　-　　-　　-　Review Editor.

W. B. GODBEY,　　Sunday-school and Question Drawer.

MRS. M. W. KNAPP,　　　Young People's Department.

OBJECT.

To promote deep spirituality among all believers.

To magnify the New Testament standard of piety and
doctrine, especially emphasizing Scriptural Regeneration
for sinners and the Baptism with the Holy Ghost for all of
God's children.

To help spread the Gospel of Bible Holiness over "all
the world."

To oppose the formality, worldliness and ecclesiastical
usurpation which threaten the very life of the believer.

To proclaim the freedom of individual conscience in
all matters not sinful.

By God's grace we hope to make it one of THE BEST
PAPERS ISSUED.

PRICE, $1.00 PER YEAR.

☞ Agents wanted everywhere.

M. W. KNAPP, Publisher,　-　　-　Cincinnati, Ohio.

LIGHTNING BOLTS FROM PENTECOSTAL SKIES,

Or, Devices of the Devil Unmasked.

By MARTIN WELLS KNAPP.

Table of Contents.

Frontispiece of Author.

Striking Illustrations designed by Author;
Executed by J. A. Knapp.

1. Struck by Lightning. 2. Lost, Saved, Fully Sanctified. 3. Diagram of Christ's Return. 4. The Rapture. 5. On the Rock and on the Sand. 6. "Three Demon Spirits Hover."

Neatly Bound.
Good Paper.
Over 300 Pages.
Price, $1.00.

DARE YOU READ IT?

THIS STRIKING BOOK and *FULL SALVATION QUARTERLY* FREE to all who send $1.00 mentioning this offer. *THREE* copies postpaid to any paid-up subscriber of The Revivalist, who will promise to send us $2.00 within thirty days from time of receiving books. ☞ Given as a premium for *three* subscribers to The Weekly Revivalist.

Other Books by this Author.

Out of Egypt Into Canaan. 24,000. 80 cents. "Able, clear, and forcible."—Central Methodist.

Christ Crowned Within. 19,000. 75 cents. "A treasury of the burning thoughts of those who lived nearest the Master."—Bishop McCabe

"Impressions." 6,000. 50 cents. "A most instructive, suggestive, and useful book.—S. A. Keen. "We advise everybody to read it."—Central Baptist.

The Double Cure. Sanctification simplified. 13,000. 10 cents.

Revival Kindlings. Revival facts and incidents. 5,000. $1.00. "I will be read with comfort and delight."—Mich. Christian Advocate.

Revival Tornadoes. 13,000. $1.00. "A keen exposure of sham Revivals."—Christian Standard.

The whole set with Lightning Bolts and The Revivalist, one year, postpaid, $5.00

Agents and Book Evangelists Wanted Everywhere.

M. W. KNAPP, Revivalist Office, Cincinnati, O.

TOUCHING INCIDENTS · · ·

. . AND . .

ı . . . REMARKABLE ANSWERS TO PRAYER.

These are valuable books, having a remarkable sale
and doing untold good.

Large Edition.

Cloth, 320 pages; price, *$1.00*. Agents making
from **$20.00** to **$30.00** per week.

Children's Edition

Has 128 pages, illustrated with forty-two cuts.
Price, *35 cents.*

Average Sales 10,500 per month

A little girl, thirteen years old, made **$7.50** in one day.
A crippled boy made **$40** in two weeks. A man made
$12.50 in one day. Others have done equally as well.
Fairly presented, **they sell themselves.**

From a multitude of Testimonials, we quote the following:

The Union Signal, organ of the W. C. T. U.: "This book is neither
doctrinal nor denominational, yet distinctly Christian. Its high religious
tone, its fascinating spirit, and the high rank of its contributors, make it
a strong faith-tonic, and an inspiration to prevailing prayer."

Michigan Christian Advocate: "The incidents are very pathetic."

Write at once for Terms to Agents.

Be early in the field. A copy of each book is all the outfit needed.
These will be sent, post-paid, on receipt of price.

.

www.ingramcontent.com/pod-product-compliance
Lightning Source LLC
Chambersburg PA
CBHW020040040426
42331CB00030B/108